ADRIFT

To order additional copies of **ADRIFT**,
by Grenville Lee Dunstan, call 1-800-765-6955.

Visit us at *www.reviewandherald.com* for more information
on Review and Herald products.

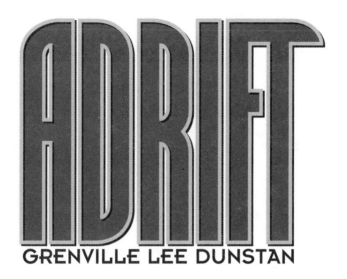

ADRIFT

GRENVILLE LEE DUNSTAN

ʀ

REVIEW AND HERALD® PUBLISHING ASSOCIATION
HAGERSTOWN, MD 21740

Texts credited to NIV are from the *Holy Bible, New International
Version*. Copyright © 1973, 1978, 1984, International Bible Society.
Used by permission of Zondervan Bible Publishers.

This book was
Edited by Gerald Wheeler
Photos by Lee Dunstan, sketches by Derrol Maisi
Cover design by Bondesign
Cover illustration by Christian Mildh
Interior design by Madelyn Ruiz
Electronic makeup by Shirley M. Bolivar
Typeset: 11/15 Veljovic

PRINTED IN U.S.A.

05 04 03 02 01   5 4 3 2 1

R&H Cataloging Service
Dunstan, Grenville Lee, 1951-
    Adrift.

    1. Survival after airplane accidents, shipwrecks,
etc.—South Pacific.
    I. Title.
                        613.69

ISBN 0-8280-1509-0

ACKNOWLEDGMENTS

Derrol Maisi

Community worker and elected councillor for the island of Emirau, Derrol Maisi provided much of the background information concerning Emirau, as well as the story itself. His help was most appreciated in organizing interviews and in helping me communicate with the surviving drifters. Derrol also provided the drawings. I wish to thank him for his hospitality and untiring help during my visit to Kavieng. This story is especially close to Derrol. His own great-grandfather was also lost at sea off Emirau Island before Derrol's birth. He was fishing from a canoe when a storm blew him out to sea. His body was never found.

Larry DaRosa, Captain of the *Evelina DaRosa*

Larry provided many of the details for the final few chapters. I'm indebted to him for his information regarding the rescue and subsequent events. Larry says he's a better fisherman than a writer, but I disagree. A generous and authentic Christian, Larry has spent 25 years on the high seas, following in the wake of his Portuguese father, who labored 40 years in fishing, and his grandfather before him, who was a whaler in the Azores.

CONTENTS

Introduction

While preparing this book, I was privileged to visit Papua New Guinea (PNG). Between flights in and out of Jacksons Airport, Port Moresby, I fell into conversation with an expatriate planter from the island of Karkar, just off the north coast of the mainland. He told me how his adult son had once retrieved a PNG national from another island near New Britain, where he'd been held captive by primitive tribespeople, who worshiped him as a god. The natives had rescued him from a large navigation buoy in the waters nearby, and taken him home to their village. He'd spent weeks in an open canoe drifting across the Bismarck Sea before reaching this one piece of civilization in the middle of the ocean, to which he clung, until the Karkar islanders found him.

In the 1970s a Manatani Islander drifted all the way to Kiribati. Not long after, a Kiribati was washed onto a reef adjacent to Utu High School, a few miles along the north coast from Kavieng, New Ireland.

Even the best-equipped and most-experienced sailors sometimes find themselves cast adrift. As I write, rescuers are plucking survivors from sunken boats in the 1998 Sydney-to-Hobart yacht race. No one, it seems, is immune to the seeming malevolence and ill-temper of nature.

Such incidents occur regularly in the wide empty expanse of the Pacific. This is the account of just one.

Some became fools through their rebellious ways

and suffered affliction because of their iniquities. . . .

Others went out on the sea in ships;

they were merchants on the mighty waters.

They saw the works of the Lord,

his wonderful deeds in the deep.

For he spoke and stirred up a tempest

that lifted high the waves.

They mounted up to the heavens

and went down to the depths;

in their peril their courage melted away.

They reeled and staggered like drunken men;

they were at their wits' end.

Then they cried out to the Lord in their trouble,

and he brought them out of their distress.

He stilled the storm to a whisper;

the waves of the sea were hushed.

They were glad when it grew calm,

and he guided them to their desired haven.

Let them give thanks to the Lord for his unfailing love

and his wonderful deeds for men.

—Ps. 107:17-31, NIV

CHAPTER
1

NO WAY HOME

They were lost and they knew it. The rise and fall of the wind-driven southerly swell and the dull, blood-red orb of the setting sun, virtually invisible in the haze-filled sky, were their only clues to the direction of Emirau Island, their destination and home.

The six young men had motored all day in their 19-foot fiberglass dingy (locally referred to as a banana boat) since early morning. A journey that should have taken just a few hours had turned into an all-day crawl. The men grumbled to Donald, one of the youngest of the group at 30 years of age. They called him the "captain," for although the boat didn't belong to him, he did own the 25-horsepower Yamaha outboard motor that powered it. It was *his* voyage, and *he* was responsible.

Donald had brought along too much cargo, the other men complained. As a result, the boat wouldn't plane, and instead of moving at upward of 15 knots, it trudged across the water at no more than five. And that had created their problem. Such a slow pace, given the undetectable currents and wind drift, made it difficult to tell how far they'd gone in the hours since they'd left Tench Island. Now they could only guess as to whether Emirau Island lay ahead, or to the left or right of them. It might even be behind them, passed by in the ocean haze that engulfed the waters of the Bismarck Archipelago, a string of islands off the north coast of Papua New Guinea (PNG).

But none of them was too worried. They couldn't be far from Emirau. Besides, Tench would have notified Emirau Island, about 40 miles due west, of their departure and given an ETA. When they failed to arrive at Emirau, aircraft and boats would come looking for them. It was just a matter of time. They had food enough—in fact, the two large bunches of bananas, *saksak* (sago) and *kaukau* (sweet potato), plus 100 pounds of other fruit and vegetables, was enough to feed six hungry men for weeks. Ironically, it was this overabundance of food that had so slowed their passage.

It was now almost sunset, and before it became too dark to see, it was necessary to do what they could to ensure their survival for the night and resume their search for home on the morrow. Between them, they had a good knowledge of the sea and how to handle themselves in such an emergency. So although they were unprepared for such a situation, they didn't see it as desperate, and merely felt annoyed about the inconvenience.

"We must make a sea anchor to slow our drift," Donald said, realizing his responsibility. "What have we got that would be suitable?"

A sea anchor usually consists of a piece of sailcloth, a car tire, or other materials that, when waterlogged, prevents a boat being blown along by the wind, thus limiting its drift to nearer the speed of the current in which it sits. It also keeps a craft headed into the wind, a more comfortable and safe way to ride out rough weather.

The men took stock of any likely materials on board. The most obvious anchor was a screwtop five-gallon plastic container. Under the jumble of cargo someone found a length of lightweight nylon rope that they tied to the container, then dropped it over the side. As it filled with water, it made a good anchor, thus slowing their fairly rapid northward drift. Without it, pushed along by the lively southeast trade wind—which appeared to be freshening—they could quickly drift outside of the likely search zone.

By the time they'd finished making the anchor, daylight had vanished. The tropics has very little twilight, so darkness comes quickly once the sun has set. Then, comfortable in the thought that they had done all they could, the six settled down, their backs resting against the fiberglass hull and their heads on the gunwales, to a restless and uncomfortable sleep. Tomorrow, someone would find them.

~

"Would you like to go home for the weekend?" Donald had called earlier that day from his boat to the group of men sitting on the cement-and-coral seawall of Kavieng's Nusa Harbor. "I'm going to Tench this afternoon, stopping there Saturday, then on to Emirau Sunday morning."

With plenty of time on their hands, as they were all basically unemployed, it was easy to agree. Kavieng town didn't have much going on despite its status as the provincial and commercial center of New Ireland Province. Extensive copra and cocoa plantations occupy almost every mile of the narrow coastal strip of the elongated, pencil-thin island. And, like much of Papua New Guinea, it is largely a subsistence culture in which regular employment is rare—and then only for the better educated.

It had taken little persuading from Donald for his *wantoks* (WUN-tork, or extended family) to accept his offer. Besides their company, he hoped that perhaps they would contribute something toward the cost of the gas and two-stroke engine oil that powered his outboard motor.

All six of the men had roots planted deep in the soil of Emirau Island, so were keen to get back and spend time with their families. The six-mile long island of Emirau is one of the St. Matthias Group, which also included the larger Mussau Island at around 300 square miles, and Tench Island—tiny with less than one square mile of inhabitable land. Except for a few of the younger people, all of the island's inhabitants are Seventh-day Adventists.

Donald James assumed the role of boat "captain" as they bolted his motor to the boat's transom. The second youngest of the group and something of an entrepreneur, he used the banana boat, which belonged to a policeman friend in Kavieng, to fish for sharks in the deep waters off New Ireland. He sold their fins for shark-fin soup, an expensive, sought-after delicacy in some quarters. Often he carried small amounts of cargo from island to island, and so with a lifetime on the water, felt completely comfortable making the relatively short trip between Kavieng, at the northern tip of New Ireland, across the Ysabel Channel to Emirau, the most northerly land of PNG and just two degrees south of the equator. He was in Kavieng doing a bit of trading when he'd met his *wantoks*.

Grosby Ume was a tall and strong youth with a gentle disposition and manner of speaking that contrasted with his rather intimidating appearance. His father was a local church leader who worked on one of several copra plantations on Emirau. A staunch member of the Seventh-day Adventist Church, Ume had a strong belief in God's providence and His care over those who trusted in Him.

In contrast to Grosby, 20-year-old Cleveland Kolivoso was of lighter build and carried less weight. His father had been a church minister, but had died soon after retiring. Following his father's death Cleveland lived with various uncles on Emirau and in Kavieng. But lacking the attention and discipline of a true father, he began to get into mischief. Although he still attended church, recently things had started to go bad. When the offering from the Leoa Seventh-day Adventist Church on Emirau disappeared, rumors circulated that Cleveland had been involved. The accusation hung heavily over him during the months afterward.

The third member of the crew was Vince Benny. Also slightly built, he wore a short beard that gave him an untidy look. Vince's life had always revolved around the church, for his father, Benny, had been a pioneer missionary in PNG. As young men, Benny and his brother, Sikanikame, had met a Fijian missionary,

Pastor Sumbale, who encouraged the brothers to attend the Seventh-day Adventist mission school near Rabaul, New Britain—an island a day's sailing to the southeast. Eventually Benny became a teacher, and Sikanikame a pastor to their fellow Emirau Islanders.

Titus Lauvos was thickset and strong. He too had been a churchgoing lad until more recently, but yielding to peer-group pressure, he'd begun to drift away from his faith. Although he hadn't been in any real trouble, he had ignored some of the ideals and principles of his childhood church. His grandfather had also been a church pastor.

At about 40 years of age, Joses Kareke was the oldest of the men. After finishing grade 6, he'd worked in various jobs before going to the huge Bougainville Island copper mine. Then the island's secessionist terror campaign had forced its shutdown, throwing him out of work. Since then he'd labored in construction, mainly as a plumber. He was quite a handyman. Joses' trade experience, general practical knowledge, and skills would always prove invaluable when anyone needed to improvise something.

Although the general appearance of the six varied greatly, all had the same glistening dark skin and a thick mat of curly hair that protected them from the sun. While they lacked a complete formal education, all could read and lacked nothing in intelligence. As a group they would have looked at home even in Western society. Products of a transitional society, they had lost many of the traditional seafaring skills of their forefathers—skills that would have enabled them to have found their way home. Now their struggle to survive would be a difficult one.

EMIRAU ISLAND HOME

Of the 700 islands comprising Papua New Guinea, Emirau Island is among the least significant. Part of the St. Matthias Group, it sits astride the northern portal of the country, an emerald in a sapphire sea. The fact that it is barely two degrees south of the equator makes it hot and humid. Today, for the most part, its people are hospitable, law-abiding, spiritual, and contented. But behind the idyllic tranquility of the beautiful islands is a relatively short history of civilization.

Islands such as Emirau have changed dramatically in just a few generations. Some Emirau islanders even 50 years after its pacification and Christianization still remember the fear—even terror—of their former lives. They experienced the degradation of devil worship, and saw the island's population decimated by fighting, disease, and plague.

The island's indigenous population are the descendants of two principal clans—the Evele and Saitalai. Although the clans were related, they spent a lot of time fighting each other as those from the northern district united to battled those of the southern district. Things continued this way until after World War I when Australia received responsibility for administering the former German colony of New Guinea.

Papua New Guinea almost universally considers women of low status, but not Emirau. There the society is matriarchal, inheritance passing through the mother's line. Women own the two most important possessions: the land and the children. Land disputes are commonplace all through Papua New Guinea, but on Emirau, if a person gets caught trespassing or stealing from someone else's land, the mother-owner is the one who decides whether to take action—sometimes with fatal consequences—or to seek compensation.

And trespassers there are not always forgiven. A relative of the infringed family may be sent to apprehend and question the intruder, and if he finds their intentions to be less than honorable, then the relative extracts compensation, which sometimes means that he will kill the trespasser. But, as in much of PNG, one killing always deserves another, and the payback concept of justice, if not contained early, will often lead to wholesale killing in feuds that last for generations. On Emirau, if another clan ever killed a woman, outright warfare almost inevitably followed.

Stories of such lawlessness still circulate, but today, in contrast to most of PNG, these islands are quite safe and peaceful. These days the weapon of choice is the ballot box rather than machete or bow and arrow, and men vie with women for positions of leadership among the clans in political rather than military campaigns.

Emirau has seen a lot of fighting in its time, and both its landscape and people carry the scars of such conflicts. A huge concrete and asphalt runway, a product of the Second World War, slashes across the landscape. Concrete structures overgrown by vines and scattered about in awkward places litter the island. They are former bunkers and the foundations of long-demolished buildings, the relics of General Douglas Macarthur's hard-fought military campaign against the Japanese. By 1943 the Japanese army had entrenched itself in Kavieng, as well as other strategic points along Papua New Guinea's northern coast and islands, forming the picket line of the Greater East Asia Prosperity Sphere. But while the derelict fortifications and rusting structures continue to hamper commercial and subsistence cultivation on the island, the lengthy and well-constructed runway has proved to be a boon to communication in recent years. The runway is sufficiently long and heavy to land light commercial jets operated by the country's national carrier, Air Niuguni. So in addition to the commuter services of small-plane operators, convenient and fast-jet services connect the island to Port Moresby, the nation's capital about two hours flying time across the Bismarck Sea to the south.

U.S. Army Seabees constructed two runways during the latter part of the war. The first and smaller consists of corimace, or crushed coral. Its purpose was to get men and their equipment onto the ground, and to provide a runway for the fighter planes that protected them while they built the second longer, heavy-duty strip for heavy bombers and transports. At its peak the tiny island had six operational airstrips. Although Australian teams attempted a cleanup after the war, the remains of the American presence still cover the island. Souvenir hunters armed with metal detectors, and tourists, including many former U.S. servicemen and their families, often find relics of the conflict as they roam the jungle or walk the beaches.

The presence of the massive airstrip and the island's almost unique position close to the equator has also prompted interest in the island by space agencies seeking a site for an alternative spaceport to the French Ariane facility, also about the same distance north of the equator in French Guiana, South America.

Seeking to build the world's first fully commercial spaceport for launching large satellites for radio and telephone communication, directors of an Australian space industries company, along with executives of major construction enterprises, recently accompanied officials from Russia's space industry to the island for an evaluation. Only a relatively few such secure and accessible launch sites exist along the equator.

At the equator the earth's speed of rotation is at its greatest, producing a slingshot effect for rocket launches. The extra speed enables a more economical launch into space as the rockets can either carry a heavier payload or use less fuel to thrust a satellite into orbit. Unlike surveillance, spy, and research satellites, for example, that often have a north-south orientation, communication satellites always require a geostationary orbit much deeper in space and directly above the equator. And with much of the potential site on Emirau already rendered useless for commercial agriculture by the concrete and asphalt left over from the war, Emirau has little to lose and so hopes the project will go ahead. Emirau itself could soon be launched direct from the Stone Age to the Space Age.

Just a few yards off Emirau's azure lagoons and coconut-fringed beaches one finds numerous ship and plane wrecks dating from the war, while beautiful reefs teem with hundreds of varieties of exotic fish. The latter serve as the destination for the tourists, deep-sea fishers, and scuba and skindivers who arrive aboard luxury yachts each year. Such often well-heeled aquatic adventurers are intent on catching "the big one" or relaxing 100 feet down in the indigo depths of a benign Pacific. They bring hard currency, economic development, and services to an otherwise neglected and sleepy backwater of Papua New Guinea.

The fishing and dive boats bristle with long rods and antennae. They are equipped with the latest and best in luxury—IDD satellite telephone, freshwater showers, air-conditioning, bars below decks—and safety, including EPIRB homing devices, GPS navigation and radar, aids that Donald and his fellow castaways must have wished that they also had. And after a weekend or week of fishing, snorkeling, or scuba diving the reefs, the visitors could return to the clean convenience of some place such as the classy Malagan Lodge on Kavieng's quaint and romantic harbor-front.

Kavieng town, where the six young men had lived before setting off for Emirua, had been heavily fortified by the Japanese during the war. A strategic naval and air base, its defenses had been strong. Just a few meters from the modest front door of the upscale Malagan Resort are tunnels burrowed into the cliff face, and nearby lie huge chunks of concrete from bombed and shelled pillboxes, storage facilities, and antiaircraft emplacements. A short distance along the beachfront are large swivelling naval guns mounted on massive concrete foundations. They rust away beneath a permanent camouflage of vines in the shade of overhanging coconut palms.

Kavieng was one spoke in the Japanese' southwest Pacific defensive wheel of which Rabaul, New Britain, was the hub. Like Rabaul's Simpson Harbor that guarded the St George's Channel between New Ireland and New Britain, Kavieng's Nusa Harbor protected Steffen Strait and Ysabel Channel, the northern entrances into the Bismarck Sea. They were also transhipment points for the naval and merchant marine forces and supply bases for the ground forces on New Guinea's north coast. Rabaul was the principal command center of Japanese operations for the entire southwest Pacific and endured continual pounding by U.S. carrier-based, and later, land-based bombers.

Admiral Yamamoto, Japanese supreme commander of the Pacific theater, had his underground headquarters bunker in Rabaul (although it is somewhat deeper underground since a recent volcanic eruption), and for many years, as a small decrepit museum, was a significant tourist attraction. A few miles inland from Rabaul, near the Seventh-day Adventist training college at Sonoma, is another labyrinth of tunnels. This massive system is like a multilevel railroad switching yard with branching and rejoining lines of tunnels. It was the communication center for the Imperial Japanese Air Force in that theater. Nearby are a number of former fighter-bomber strips.

American forces, following General Macarthur's plan to minimize U.S. casualties by avoiding any direct head-on confrontations with the Japanese where possible, bypassed both Rabaul and Kavieng and constructed their own air and naval bases rather than attempting to capture the heavily fortified airstrips and hardened Japanese naval bases as they did on Guadalcanal. But to be safe from attack by Kavieng-based planes and to neutralize its effectiveness as a supply center, the Allies did have to attack its airfield and port facilities.

It was during one such attack in February 1944 that one of the most noteworthy acts of courage of the Pacific theater occurred. For three days B-24, B-25, and A-20 bombers mauled Kavieng. The bombers repeatedly hit the airfield and fuel dumps located a few miles inland from Kavieng. A number of U.S. planes hit by antiaircraft fire had to ditch into the harbor, within clear view of Japanese shore batteries. A downed B-24 crew from the 345th Bomb Group bobbed helplessly in life rafts and came under fire. They knew their only chance of survival was a rescue attempt by a PBY Catalina flying boat.

Flying cover for the raid on February 15 was 28-year-old Lt. Nathan Gordon. He gets two lines in *United States Aviation*. They read: "Gordon, Nathan, G. Lt. (Jg) USN 11421 Rescue of 15 officers and men under heavy fire in Kavieng Harbor, 15 Feb 1944."

Disregarding the heavy enemy fire, he put his PBY down in the harbor by what turned out to be merely an empty raft. Then he radioed to a second raft closer to shore, where he began to attract enemy fire, but managed to pick up the airmen. He took off, but then another call came, so he touched down again and dragged three more aboard. Now he was overloaded, but just as he was about to head back to base, he received yet another plea for help. This time he picked up six more drifting men just 1,000 yards from the hostile shoreline. Each time he had to cut his motors to enable his crew to pull the bobbing, unsteerable rafts filled with men aboard.

It's not surprising, then, that Lieutenant Gordon's entry in *Aviation* comes under the heading: "Medal of Honor Awards." His Medal of Honor citation ends with these words: "By his exceptional daring, personal valor, and incomparable airmanship under the most perilous conditions, Lt Gordon prevented certain death or capture of airmen by the Japanese."

A few days later, on March 20, 1944, an American force occupied Emirau. It eventually totaled some 40,000 servicemen and women and heralded the beginning of the encirclement of the Japanese on New Ireland and New Britain and an end to Japanese domination of the Bismarck Sea and the northern coast of mainland New Guinea. The military shipped most of the islanders to nearby Mussau Island until the war ended.

But many of the indigenous people of New Ireland became quite fond of their American liberators. They identified them with a seemingly inexhaustible supply of supplies, or "cargo" as such shipments are known locally. In other places around the South Pacific this amazing flow of wealth from the air gave rise to "cargo cults" that developed into a new religion. For many years afterward the villagers fervently prayed for (and expected) the return of the Americans and their wealth.

The people of New Hanover, a large island visible on the horizon to the west of Kavieng, certainly didn't forget their American friends. They chose former U.S. President Lyndon B. Johnson as their candidate in the election for the first Papua New Guinea Parliament during the late 1960s. To reinforce their demand for LBJ, they refused to hand over their taxes to authorities, instead using the money to establish a fund to buy him!

New Ireland itself has the longest record of contact with Europeans of all South Pacific cultures. Well before James Cook sailed to Tahiti and Tasman found New Zealand, Dutch explorers and merchants from the Spice Islands (present day Indonesia) further to the west sailed its waters. Later, Germany sought colonies for trade and the prestige of an empire, and claimed the northern half of what is now mainland Papua New Guinea and its islands to its north. In the late 1800s German planters arrived and began to convert the narrow coastal strip and low offshore islands to copra (coconut), cocoa, palm oil, and rubber production. Lutheran and Catholic German missionaries began to Christianize the New Guinea nationals.

William Dampier sighted and named the St. Matthias Islands in 1700. With the arrival and occupation of the islands by Europeans after 1864, plantation recruiters came looking for labor, a practice that gradually depopulated the outer islands. While much of the island culture and way of life has succumbed to Europeanization, it's not all gone. You can still glimpse it around Kavieng. In the protected waters of Nusa Harbor dark-skinned, woolly-haired islanders ply the calm waters in hand-built dugout canoes laden with fish and coconuts, the family groceries for the next week, children, and, on occasion, the adventurous tourist. Traditionally the canoes were outrigger in style, their islander crews navigating the open sea by sun and stars and the interplay of the wind-driven waves and counter-swells that move continuously and inexorably across the endless ocean.

Life in those days, at least in the towns of New Ireland, was relatively good. The German planters and traders prospered as a result of the demand for their products in Europe. By contrast, up until the 1930s, the islands of the nearby St. Matthias group remained largely isolated. They had an unenviable reputation as being so underdeveloped, unhealthy, and dominated by pagan practices that Europeans considered them off limits to all but the hardy administrators who had to make periodic visits. Through the years a number of Europeans died trying to establish themselves on plantations on the islands.

At that time only about 500 people lived on Emirau. Although the authorities considered them "friendly," it still viewed them as savages who lived a degraded lifestyle in abject conditions. They were "filthy, covered with sores, eating all kinds of unclean foods, and following many vices," wrote author A. W. Spalding. "They were so miserable and outcast that the government considered them beyond help, and looked only for them to die out." One medical officer who visited in 1922 reported the Emirau people as "singing their Swan Song with malaria," that had been "allowed to become murderous by neglect."

In the late 1920s an epidemic of polio swept through Mussau, and allegedly took the lives of 230 people. Then things began to get better. In 1929 the Seventh-day Adventist Church, a relative fledgling in the Pacific in regard to missions, began to change the pagan practices and physical degradation of the Emirau people. A Solomon Islands missionary, Oti Maekera, spearheaded the transformation. The church's impact eventually led the medical officer who had pessimistically prophesied the extinction of the Emirau people to report that the arrival of the "Seven-days" was "about the best thing that ever happened" to the people of the St. Matthias group.

Oti arrived on the church-owned ketch MV *Veilomani* under the command of a Captain G. McClaren. In Fijian *Veilomani* means "light." McClaren, also the superintendent of the Seventh-day Adventist mission in the region, had visited previously and vowed to return with a missionary. Now, in fulfillment of his promise, he dropped Oti on Emirau and sailed away. In his book *Christ's Last Legion* (Review and Herald, 1949), Spalding tells how Christianity transformed the lives of the people of Emirau. "He [Oti] came into a native village. There he heard a terrible commotion on the far side, and thither he went. A woman with shrill voice was crying out, while a witch doctor chanted incantations over her. Pushing his way through snarling villagers, Oti commanded silence, then explained to the crowd that Satan was troubling the woman, but he would tell them of a deliverer, Jesus Christ. Turning to the raging woman, he said, 'Do you know who I am?'

"'Yes,' she said. 'You are Oti. You have come from the Solomon Islands to tell us of Jesus. You are a Seventh-day Adventist missionary.'"

Oti then told the people: "You hear this woman. She has never seen me, but she is able to tell who I am. This is the work of Satan. I shall now pray to my God, and He will cast out the evil spirit. But you must be quiet."

Then he prayed briefly, and as the crowd remained silent, he took one step toward the woman. Raising his hand, he declared, "In the name of Jesus Christ, I command you to come out of this woman and leave her alone."

The woman shrieked as an unseen power lifted her and threw her to the ground. At first she seemed dead, but then she opened her eyes and looked around.

"Give her food and water," Oti commanded. And when she had grown stronger, he said to her, "Do you know who I am?"

"No," the woman replied, "I have never seen you before."

"But you know why I am here?"

"No, of course not. You are a stranger to me. I have never seen or heard of you before."

Then Oti preached to the crowd about the plan of salvation through Jesus, and before he left, every man and woman in that village had accepted Christ as Saviour (pp. 363, 364).

On October 20, 1931, the *Veilomani* returned to

Emirau and anchored not far from shore near the village of Leoa. From the beach the villagers could hear singing on board as the captain and his crew along with the missionaries engaged in worship. Attracted by the music, the people of Leoa demanded that the missionaries teach them to sing in a similar fashion. Captain McClaren was more than happy to do so. He not only taught them to sing, he instructed them about the love of Jesus and the freedom that a belief in God brings. Eventually they discarded their pagan ways and accepted Jesus. They cleaned themselves up, killed all their pigs, and soon produced missionaries of their own.

People were amazed at the transformation of the people of the St. Matthias islands. One official said in 1932: "I am astonished at what I have seen. I cannot realize that such a change is possible. The people have taken hold of your religion with a fervid zeal that cannot be described, but must be seen to be appreciated. . . . They are changed. They now seem to be living for something which I cannot understand. . . . I marvel, and say it is a miracle."

Within a few years almost the entire population of Emirau had converted to Christianity and become Seventh-day Adventists. Many of them went to the other parts of Papua and New Guinea, including the mainland, where they worked in the alien, isolated, and hostile highland environment, many days' travel from the familiar coastal climes in which they felt more at home. Today, most Emirau islanders follow the Christian tradition, either as practicing Seventh-day Adventists or sympathetic to it. When Captain McClaren and the

Veilomani visited Emirau, he had asked the local chief, Sousala, to give him two boys from his island to take to Rabaul to be educated. Those two boys became the father and uncle of Vince Benny, who now found himself drifting helplessly across the same waters plied by the *Veilomani* when it had brought Christianity to his ancestors. Now, on a boat of his own, Vince needed all the faith that gospel had endowed upon him. This he carried in his heart—and in a small Bible that he read to his fellow castaways to encourage them.

Because of their cultural and religious heritage, it wasn't hard for the drifting men to seek God in their peril. When the time came they would look again at God's promises and the stories of His protection in the Bible. They would read the Shepherd's Psalm (Psalm 23) with a new understanding. But unknown to them, their path would be through a long, deep, and shadow-filled valley. Despair and tragedy would test their faith to the maximum.

THE SEARCH

I n the pre-dawn gloom the men stirred from an uncomfortable night's sleep. It was Monday, August 18, 1997. Believing that their relatives would be missing them by now, they assumed that they need only wait patiently for their rescuers to come.

"How long, do you think?" Joses asked of anyone who was listening.

Donald, feeling a little defensive, answered. "Tench will radio Emirau to see if we arrived OK," he said, trying to sound optimistic. "They will probably give us a few more hours in the daylight to see if we arrive before calling Emergency Services in Kavieng. But someone will probably come looking for us before a proper search gets started. Just to be sure."

"I think that their chances of finding us are not good," Vince commented as he surveyed the ocean shrouded in a gray, early morning haze. He sniffed at the air and ran his hand across his face, pausing as he did so to rub sleep from his eyes. "This cloud isn't just a fog that will rise with the sun. It's smoke, and if we can't see through it, then neither will they."

"We will just have to get lucky," Titus said.

The men laughed hesitantly. Although they each were confident that someone would find them, the seed of a thought that the rescuers might not spot them was beginning to germinate in their minds.

"Don't count on luck. I think it would be better if we would pray," came Vince's cautionary response.

But the others weren't about to—at least not yet.

For now they could do little but await rescue. Donald had already checked the fuel in the seven-gallon tank and done some mental arithmetic. They had little fuel left, so he decided not to run the outboard motor any more, at least not in any haphazard attempt to find land. *In which direction should we head?* he thought. *There's no hope of sighting land through the haze that blankets us, especially when it is almost impossible to see the sun through it. The wind is from the south and quite fresh. Despite the sea anchor the boat would have continued to drift northward, most likely further from land. Given a rate of drift of even 1 or 2 knots, overnight, we could have gone 20 to 30 miles, well beyond the range of our remaining fuel.* He assumed they were probably already somewhere well north of Cape Siemens, the northernmost land of Papua New Guinea. *No, unless we spot another boat or an island, I will not use the motor.*

Someone tore a hand of bananas from one of two large bunches laying on the floor of the boat and handed them around. The salt air made the men hungry. They peeled the bananas and threw the skins overboard. The skins were already darkening. Contact with salt air and water does that, ripening them faster than on land. As they ate, they peered into the mist, listening for the reassuring sound of an approaching motorboat or aircraft. As soon as they heard something, they would try to attract attention. After all, they had plenty of time.

∼

Ocean air is typically haze-filled to some extent, more so than on land. But in the tropics, with its high evaporation and strong sunlight heating and distorting the air, visibility is usually less than in the temperate latitudes. Good visibility all the way to the horizon is the exception rather than the rule. Nevertheless, it is still usually measured in miles. But in August 1997, as the six drifted helplessly toward the equator, visibility both on land and at sea was now measured in yards because of an unfortunate combination of two of nature's most powerful and destructive forces: the *El Niño* effect and nearby volcanic eruptions.

As was the case with many Pacific Rim countries, *El Niño* had brought to PNG one of its worst droughts in memory. As in much of Southeast Asia, crops had failed and people were starving. It was so bad that aid organizations and the military were dropping supplies from the air to isolated island and rural communities.

El Niño severely disrupts the rainfall patterns in the western Pacific, including Australia, Indonesia, Borneo, Malaysia, and the Philippines. The usually reliable wet season fails as warm ocean currents heat the adjacent atmosphere; temperature inversions occur, and rainfall shifts away from the tropics, leaving it browned and thirsty. Hoping to capitalize on the dryness, and with little knowledge of long-range weather forecasts, subsistence farmers across the zone had attempted to establish new gardens. Using a cultivation process known as *swidden,* or slash-and-burn farming, farmers start fires to clear the normally damp jungle in preparation for planting. Add to this indiscriminate burning by vandals and bored locals, and soon a pall of semi-translucent smoke drifted listlessly across thousands of square miles.

In some places the smoke was so dense that commercial aircraft had to alter their flight paths, and some airports, including Singapore's busy Changi International Airport, had to temporarily shut down. For those planes not equipped with radar, much of Southeast Asia and PNG was a no-fly zone. On mainland PNG, where the smoke was worst, light planes remained grounded for days as their pilots waited for a clear sky.

Across the Bismarck Sea, some 200 miles southeast of where the men now bobbed awaiting rescue, two small hills, sentinels on the approaches to the beautiful Simpson Harbor, Rabaul, were literally blowing their tops. The hills—Matupit and Vulcan—are two of a number of volcanoes near Rabaul. And since they'd first exploded in a fantastic pyroclastic display in 1994, they'd continued to eject tons of ash, dust, and debris thousands of feet skyward, creating some fantastically beautiful sunsets in the region, shrouding the area in smoke.

The volcanoes are almost on the edge of Rabaul, the New Britain provincial center. They ejected so much debris that the population eventually abandoned the town and left it to be buried. The town's northeastern precinct, close by Matupit, a once-thriving commercial and residential area, already lies beneath roof-height debris. As the heavy ash piled high on homes, churches, and shops, they began to collapse. Underground, the expanding caldera buckled the land surface, twisting and tearing apart even steel-framed buildings.

To visit Rabaul today is to walk into some surreal lunar landscape resembling Hiroshima following the atomic blast. It is gray, eerie, and devastated, and devoid of permanent human or animal life. The only movement in the blasted, colorless landscape is the gentle flapping of a protruding piece of rusted metal roofing in the wind. Occasionally a bird will fly overhead, but they never alight. A battered Japanese pickup, its windows missing and roof half caved in, raises dust as it traverses a bulldozed path, perhaps six or eight feet above what was once a paved road.

With only the roots of a few hardy acid-rain resistant shrubs to hold it together, the dust constantly swirls in the wind. It rises to invade every cavity of your vehicle, belongings, clothing, and person. The ash carried northwest on the trade winds added to the smoke and ocean haze that reduced visibility and prevented the six Emirauans from seeing their landfall.

~

The tepid morning quickly turned torrid as the blood-red sun rose higher. The banana boat was completely open, with no superstructure or deck at all, so it offered no protection from the dehydrating heat. Other than a couple tarpaulin-like plastic sheets protecting the cargo and some blankets, it contained nothing that they could use to keep off either weather or sun. The men were becoming just a little thirsty too. They regretted not having brought a good supply of fresh water for their half-day journey from Tench to Emirau, but who on Tench could have spared any? They made do with the bananas and fruit. But for how long? Soon they would need fresh water.

On Emirau friends and family had already raised the alarm. The six men were well overdue, and the islanders assumed that they were in trouble. If they'd suffered either a mechanical breakdown or were simply lost in the haze, Emergency Services in Kavieng must be notified.

A radio message had told Emirau that the men left Tench in the morning, expecting to reach home by 3:00 p.m. When sunset came and they still hadn't arrived, people began to worry and immediately attempted to raise Kavieng via VHF radio. Kavieng failed to respond, as they'd closed for the night, losing valuable hours for search preparation.

Monday morning Emirau finally contacted Kavieng, but it took the rest of the day to obtain authorization for a charter and to pull a plane from its scheduled commercial service. Not until Tuesday morning did the air search begin. Meanwhile, the currents pushed the boat further north. It probably was more than 100 miles north of Emirau before anyone began looking for it. Every hour that passed added hundreds more square miles to the search zone, and further reduced the odds of discovering the vessel.

With little to do but sit, talk, and think, the drifters had a chance to reflect on the ironies of their situation. They had a huge amount of food. It would last them for weeks if they weren't rescued, but in part they blamed it for their predicament. On the previous Friday they'd been able to navigate to infinitesimal Tench, a mere dot on the map and well over the horizon from Kavieng, but now they were unable to find the many-times larger Emirau or Mussau Islands.

During their Saturday stopover they had talked to Airekatia, a Tench islander, about his own experience of being lost at sea in these same waters.

He'd been fishing from his dugout canoe when a storm blew up and carried him south from Tench out into the Bismarck Sea. The New Ireland, St. Matthias, and Admiralty groups of islands border the Bismarck Sea to the north and northwest, and the New Guinea mainland and New Britain to the south and southeast. As the sea is thus somewhat enclosed, his chances of making landfall were good. It had taken him almost two months to do so, but eventually he'd washed ashore on the Gazelle Peninsula near Rabaul.

During that time, he said, he'd had virtually nothing to eat. Survival on the high seas, he told them, depended on just one thing: water. During his time adrift, which had been some years previous, it had rained most of the time, and collecting water in his canoe hull was relatively easy.

He told the men that he could tell when he was near an island, even when he couldn't see it. He would watch the smaller seabirds. Each morning they would fly out to sea looking for fish; then, toward dusk, they would return, flying in the opposite direction back to land and a place to rest.

As they ate some more of the fruit, the six men discussed what Airekatia had told them, and they wondered if such information would suddenly prove useful to them. They hoped not, preferring to be rescued first. The day drifted past until eventually the sun set and the cooler evening enveloped them. Even though they were more than a little uncomfortable, they managed to drop off to sleep.

In Kavieng the authorities finally authorized and planned the search. It would begin at sunrise Tuesday. A Kavieng-based pilot, Captain Gilmore Lavaro, flew for a small feeder airline. Although from Mussau, he had married an Emirau girl, so knew some of the families involved. As soon as he heard of the missing islanders, he volunteered his services. Eventually he obtained a plane and at first light Tuesday morning took off, headed for the Emirau search zone. On board he had spotters who searched the waters below while he flew. For as long as his fuel lasted the plane scooted back and forth across the sea. Visibility was still poor, so they had to fly low, limiting the distance they could scan, although directly below they could see the foam on the crests of the rolling Pacific Ocean swells. The wind was strengthening.

The plane crisscrossed in an ever-enlarging pattern. Because they knew the local winds and currents well, they had a good idea of where to look for the boat, and on Tuesday, about midafternoon, the men heard the drone of the low-flying search plane. As soon as they heard it approach a little closer, perhaps on the next pass, they would light a flare. If the searchers got within vision, they couldn't miss it. And if the plane flew directly overhead, it would not miss the bright orange tarpaulin spread across their cargo.

But it did. The closest the plane came was about a mile. The men could hear it pass them by, invisible through the haze. Close enough to hear, but not enough for them to set the flare or wave the tarpaulin.

Emergency Services couldn't afford to search indefinitely. The plane, being privately owned, was expensive to hire and was also needed for regular commercial air services. After two days of futile searching, and despite his willingness to continue, Emergency Services told the pilot to quit. He'd looked in all the right places and the men were not there. They couldn't have missed it, even in the haze, so they assumed the boat must have capsized and sunk.

However, at his own expense and using members of the men's families as spotters, Captain Lavaro continued to search between scheduled flights for one more day, then reluctantly had to give it up. The seas by now were quite rough, so searching in small boats was not an option. After a few days when the weather had abated, some Emirau people commandeered a boat to continue the search to the south and further west toward Manus Island, hoping to find either the men or some flotsam that might give a clue to their fate.

The men didn't hear the plane again after that first day. They had a small FM radio with them and could hear the reports of the search. Eventually an announcement said that the authorities had called it off, so they resigned themselves to a long stay at sea and set about organizing themselves for it.

Although they remained unfazed by their circumstances, if they'd known what lay ahead of them, they might have worried. They talked with optimism of the prospects of sailing to the Philippines or Taiwan, not realizing the huge distance that lay between them and such destinations. None of the six had done very well in geography at school. In fact, none of them had done much geography at all!

The school system in Papua New Guinea is highly selective. While it guarantees children a basic education, in more remote situations, such as in the highlands or on Emirau, that can still be fairly rudimentary. Most children will have finished their education at the end of grade 6. Of all the students who successfully complete grade 6, only a relatively small proportion continue on to grade 10. And of them, merely a handful are accepted into grade 11, and then only an elite (and very bright) minority go on to college.

For all aboard Donald's boat, education had pretty much stopped at the end of grade 6. That's why, when they finally pulled their sea anchor back on board after accepting the fact that they would not be found, they assumed it would be quite an easy task to sail to China—if the winds were right! As much as they loved and knew the sea and were at home in it, they had little idea of where, if blown in any given direction, they might make a landfall. No more idea, in fact, than they knew where or how long it would be when they would.

Other than due south, the nearest land of any consequence was Indonesia, some 25° to the west and 10° to the north—at least 2,000 miles—of their position. Japan, the nearest large piece of land in the direction they were now headed, was almost 2,500 miles distant. If the wind changed and blew them east, then it was Central America, a third of a world away. Of course, in between, lie scores of inhabited islands, but the chance of finding one, as they'd discovered to their chagrin, was negligible. Maybe it was best that they didn't have much idea of what most likely awaited them. But being young and optimistic they didn't contemplate anything but a safe landfall.

Their families hadn't given up. A wind change could blow them home as readily as it was sending them away. The seas had been rough, but not enough to sink them, and the search parties hadn't seen anything to indicate that. From what they'd been told by the people on Tench, the men had plenty of food on board, although they were worried because of their lack of water. They felt sure that the men were safe because the six were strong and had been taught to have faith in God. While family members recognized that all of the men didn't possess their faith, they believed that God could save them despite that. He would not desert them, so the families prayed and asked God to return their men safely. On board the little boat the men began to pray too.

～

After a week of merely drifting, and aware that the authorities had called off the search, the six men decided to take control of their destiny. They would make a sail and put the drifting boat under their control. Their food supply had diminished rapidly, as almost all the bananas had now been either eaten or become so overripe that they'd tossed them overboard. Now they were thinking they might be in for a long voyage, one in which they would need all of the remaining food plus all of the courage, mental and physical strength, initiative, and skills of seamanship they could muster.

Realizing that they couldn't sit idly day after day ignoring the prospect of a long journey, they began to sort through their cargo and found some more lightweight rope that they used to lash oars on each side of the boat, then tied the cargo tarpaulin between them. Braced with more rope as stays, they created an effective square-rigged, spinnaker-style sail. When they dropped the outboard motor leg over the transom to use as a rudder, the prow of the boat turned downwind and the craft picked up speed.

"So we will follow the wind," Vince announced when they were underway. "We will sail to China if we have to!" After almost a week of almost aimless drifting, to have some control over their direction made them all feel good. They were optimistic that they really could reach China.

CHAPTER
4

AN ILL WIND BLOWS

By the time the men hoisted their sail, they'd probably already drifted north of the equator as a result of the constant and strong southerly. Then, toward the end of their first week under sail, the wind began to pick up. The rapid shifts in its direction warned them that a storm was approaching. On Friday, when the waves began to steepen, the men stowed their sail and prepared for the worst.

The storm itself hit on Saturday. The wind had risen to gale force and shapeless clouds darkened the sky. By midafternoon they were in the midst of a full-blown tropical storm. The rain fell in huge drops, blown almost horizontal by the wind, dousing the crew who were without protection of any sort. *At least it isn't cold,* they thought to themselves.

The storm lasted four days, becoming harder to endure during darkness. Waves smashed the boat from all sides and flung it about. Unable to keep the prow into the wind, they were not always in the best attitude to ride the waves. Spume blew from the wave crests and stung their tired eyes. As they wallowed in the troughs and the whitecaps of invisible waves appeared above them, they feared they'd be swamped. Each time they rose to the crest of a wave, they then worried that they would capsize. Inch by inch the hull began to fill from the rain, spray, and breaking waves until it sloshed around their feet.

They had trouble bailing the water because of the bags of kaukau, bananas, and other cargo on the floor. They had no buckets either, and during the night it was almost impossible to bail. They ended up sitting in water up to their waists. As the storm strengthened, they found themselves tossed and slewed about at the mercy of the wind and waves. Eventually the hull contained so much water that to keep from sinking they slipped overboard and steadied the boat by clinging to the sides. They had to keep it upright and with sufficient freeboard to prevent the motor from going under. A total capsize or immersion would end the motor's usefulness, as they had no tools to dismantle and dry it. They would also lose what remained of their food supply.

To ride out the storm by hanging onto the side of the boat with their bodies half-submerged might have seemed foolhardy, but the ocean was their second home. They'd grown up playing and working in and on the sea, so they were neither afraid of it nor of what it might contain. The storm wouldn't last forever, and they had total confidence in their ability to swim through the restless green—and survive. It was what lay beyond that that worried them.

Through the night the six shouted encouragement to

each other, reassuring each other that they were still there. Eventually, as the seas subsided, they clambered back into the partially submerged hull. They sat semi-submerged for three days until sometime the next Tuesday, when the wind and seas dropped enough for them to bail the boat. They bailed it completely then set the sail, once again feeling they were in control of their destiny.

They wondered if that was to be their lot: storm and calm, followed by still another storm and calm. As they thought about it, they decided to take precautions to prevent the boat sinking in the next storm to come their way. For the moment they were still fit enough to combat the sea. But the swirling water had washed some of their food overboard and damaged the rest—and they had virtually no fresh water. They might not have the strength to outlast another storm.

The sea remained relatively calm for the next few days and by Thursday the swells had lengthened and the wind, still from the south, had moderated. They ate the last of the edible bananas and regretfully threw quite a lot of salt-affected rotting bunches overboard. It concerned them since the food, as well as being nourishing, was about 70 percent water and kept their bodies from total dehydration. Now they would lack even that source of water.

Under sail once again, they kept their northward course, always with the wind behind them. There was little to do except talk. Most of the time they simply rested their weakened bodies, half dozing as the sun and the motion of the waves lulled them to sleep.

Late one afternoon toward the end of their second

week all except Donald at the tiller, were resting, still exhausted from the storm earlier in the week. In the peace of the moment, he too was relaxed. He gazed ahead to the endless horizon, wondering where they would make landfall. *With no compass or map, and with no knowledge of the ocean in which we're sailing, what does it matter which way we head. A little this way, a little that— it is impossible to steer a course—we just follow the wind. It would be pure luck if the wind and current carried us to within grasp of rescue. If it pushes us to the vast Pacific in the east—well, that could be trouble, but if we head west, then it will take us near the Philippines, and that would be good. But there's no point in worrying or complaining. We are totally at the mercy of the wind.*

Then, in the midst of his daydream, something in the water just ahead startled Donald. The water began to heave and flow until, with a rush, a huge glistening creature emerged, languidly rolling onto its side, followed by a massive tail. The tail rose high above him, then slapped the ocean surface with a crack.

Donald turned the motor sharply, allowing the leviathan to pass a few yards from their bow. A few yards closer and the whale might have capsized them. He looked in disbelief and wonder.

"Kirap! Kirap! Lukim, olgeta!" Donald stammered to his slumbering companions. "Wake up! Wake up! Look over there, everyone!"

The men struggled from their lethargy and sat up staring about them. "It's a whale. And there's another one," Titus said, pointing to the water spout off their beam. "They always travel in groups or herds."

An Ill Wind Blows

The whales surfaced briefly before disappearing into the deep for five minutes, then reappeared another 100 yards ahead. The danger passed, but all realized that one of the huge flukes could have easily smashed their flimsy craft and killed them. The whales appeared to be on much the same course as the men—due north.

"At least they seem to know where they're going," Vince observed.

"Which is more than we do!" someone answered.

"But we are alive, and for that we can still be thankful," a third responded. "We came *so* close to being swamped."

The calm weather had lasted about four days when the wind freshened once again. The seas shortened and the waves became steeper. "It looks like another storm," Donald commented, watching a line of clouds near the horizon. "It will hit within a few hours. Let's make ready for it!" They lowered their sail and stowed it. What little else they had they fastened down securely. Whale watching was over.

The squall hit with a blast late Friday evening. It was everything as bad as what they'd experienced previously. Again the water gushed into their unprotected boat. The wind tried to blow them off the wave crests and the rollers, hitting them broadside, threatened to splinter their tiny craft.

How can we take any more? they thought as they bailed furiously.

Trouble always seems to come at night or when you are already at your most vulnerable. The storm reached its zenith in the darkness. The wind they estimated at more than 40 knots. As they sat in water up to their waists, a larger than usual wave crested right beneath them, yawing the boat about, broadside to the inrushing waves. It broached, pitching them once again into the black sea.

They clung to their boat and amazingly it stayed right side up, probably thanks to its half-filled hull, which made it too heavy for the waves to throw around easily. They stayed in the water for some hours until the seas abated a little and then crawled back aboard. As morning approached, the sea calmed enough for them to bail out the boat.

By now they really feared another storm. Although they'd been adrift for only two weeks they had already experienced two. How could they survive another? They decided to take some precautions. On board they had a number of plastic floats used on fishing nets. The floats were all over the Pacific, and during their weeks adrift, they picked up many more. First they managed to string the floats together on some line like pearls on a necklace, then they attached it to the waist of the boat like a lifebelt. Strangely enough, they would not have another major storm—but the floats would still prove useful in other ways.

The end of the second storm coincided with the last of their food supply. One problem always seemed to replace another, but that was how the rest of the voyage would be.

Bothered that they had so little control over their craft, they decided it needed some form of keel or centerboard arrangement to enable them to steer away from the wind. Even if they couldn't tack, they must have more maneuverability. They attempted to jerry-rig a keel, but without success. Their inventiveness and resources weren't sufficient and, to their chagrin, they were never successful in fashioning a keel.

On the Thursday of their third week adrift, the men's hopes received a boost. Directly overhead, glinting in the sun, were jets heading south. One after another they crossed the sky. Their boat had probably drifted under the flight path of Australia-bound traffic heading to Sydney from Seoul in Korea, or from Osaka or Tokyo in Japan.

The silver birds would silently appear, then a minute or two later they would hear the sound of the engines. By then the planes were merely specks, almost out of sight toward the southern horizon. In the time it took a plane to traverse the arc of sky, the men in their boat might have traveled half a mile at best. They knew that from such an altitude their boat would be merely a speck in the endless sea of blue and that no one would spot them. But the sight of the aircraft still encouraged them.

For another week the boat continued its inexorable drift northward, always following the wind. Although hunger and thirst now tormented them more than ever, the men were still strong and healthy, and despite having no real knowledge of where they actually were on the huge ocean, they still felt confident that they would make it to China!

And if the wind had kept up, they very well might have. Except for the periods during the storm and their initial delay in rigging a sail because they expected to be immediately rescued, they'd been under sail about two weeks. The wind had been consistent and strong. Drifting at a conservative 2 mph, then, they could easily have averaged 50 miles per day. At that rate they would be as much as 750 miles north of their starting point near Emirau and well inside the U.S. Trust Territory of the Carolinas. Within as few as three or four degrees latitude (250 miles) was Guam, the halfway navigation point for cross-Pacific air traffic. It would have been planes routed across Guam that they'd seen flying south. But other than Guam the nearest land was the small island of Truk, at about the same distance, or Palau, some 1,000 miles northwest. Their chances of finding a landfall on one of them were slim. All were merely names on a map, barely large enough to warrant a dot. However, around them there were fishing and cargo boats, improving their chances of rescue slightly.

But now they were totally without water and food. They began to sip minuscule quantities of saltwater to assuage their thirst. All day as they sat talking, they searched the horizon for boats or an elusive coconut to satisfy their growing thirst.

On Emirau coconuts were plentiful. All you had to do for a drink was shinny up a coconut palm, hack off one of the large, green nuts with a machete, and let it fall to the ground. You took your razor-sharp bush knife and with three of four blows hacked one end off. The sweet *kulau* juice—the coconut milk—splashed out as you did so, and as you raised it to your mouth to gulp a long draft, the juice trickled from around the corners of your mouth and in rivulets ran down your beard. Satisfied, you tossed the half-drunk shell into the bush.

Then you wiped your chin with the back of your hand and continued on. You never thought anything of it—until now.

But the six thirsty drifters would never take a coconut for granted again. Ever. That's all they thought about. Along the beaches of Emirau the nuts lay everywhere, washed ashore after traveling a few yards or hundreds of miles across the ocean. Sometimes they'd been in the water for so long that barnacles and weed had taken root on them. You never bothered to take one of those. But if only they could find one now. *If only!*

They saw nothing and found no thirst-quenching nuts as for the fourth week they drifted northward. By now they must have been close to Guam. It was Wednesday, and across the waves they heard the sound of a motor. It was not far away and getting louder. Yet it wasn't a boat and sounded quite different than the high-flying jets. Then they saw it. Coming toward them, just a few hundred feet above the swells, was a large aircraft. Resembling one of the four propeller-engined Dash-7s used by Air Niugini, it was flying south. Instantly all leapt to their feet and began to wave frantically. Donald was busy striking a flare. *We must be seen. The plane is so low that the pilot can't help but see us!*

But they had no time to set off the flare and at a lazy speed the plane continued on its course, perhaps half a mile away. Soon it was out of sight, then, heartbreakingly, out of hearing. The men slumped back into the boat, dejected, weakened by the sudden exertion and consequent disappointment. That had been their best chance yet, and it had slipped past them.

But, they finally reassured themselves, if they saw one plane, they would see another. Someone would spot them sooner or later. They would make it. Gradually they settled back into their monotonous routine of watching the waves rise and fall, of thinking about food and *kulau*. Their only challenge was to keep their craft on a steady course, riding the swells, pushed along by the wind. Although the chance encounter had been a huge disappointment, they thanked God that they still had their lives and prayed for eventual rescue.

And rescue once again looked a real prospect just two days later when over the horizon, loaded high with logs, came a rusty, ill-kept cargo vessel. As it approached, they did their best to steer toward it. But without keel or centerboard, it remained a futile exercise. The boat simply turned sideways to the wind and continued to slip in the same direction, pushed across the ocean's surface. They waved their shirts and shouted, trying to attract attention, but they saw no one aboard the freighter and as with the airplane, it appeared that no one noticed them.

Even if they had been seen, they were ignored. But that shouldn't have surprised them. The Celebes and South China Seas weren't so far to the west and northwest. Around the Moluccas and Philippines the sea bristles with modern-day pirates. The ruthless, heavily armed gangs use fast speedboats to chase plodding freighters, which they board, then rob or kidnap the crew. Usually they make their raids at night when they can approach unobserved off the ship's stern. Someone throws a grappling line over the railing, then the invaders stealthily haul themselves aboard. During daylight they use ploys. For example, they might pretend to be "boat people"—refugees heading south from China or Vietnam—or castaways from a shipwreck, drifters—just like the six of them. Once a boat stops to render assistance, it is easy to pull weapons from their hiding places beneath the covers and temporarily take over a lightly defended, unsuspecting steamer crew. No boat ever stops to help in those parts.

By now they'd been close to rescue three times. They'd seen planes and a boat that should have, even must have, seen them. But each time the opportunity eluded them. Gradually their thoughts began to turn to the thought that God might be their only means to salvation.

Dispirited, they once again settled back into boredom. Not surprisingly, they had little to do. Taking turns, they kept watch from the prow, trimmed the sail, or sat in the stern and steered. The most interesting pastime was fishing, even when they weren't catching anything!

~

After a day or two of relative calm, the winds shifted to more easterly. The southeast trades, as they came under the influence of the massive summertime low over Asia, were turning monsoonal, sucking them westward toward the Philippines about 2,000 miles away. They had no alternative but to follow the wind, so the prospect of China began to fade as they turned their bow on a new course toward the setting sun.

Of course they didn't know it, but the easterly would carry them toward Palau, beyond which there was absolutely nothing until the Philippines. Each day took them further from the heavier sea and air traffic around Guam and the odds of discovery diminished. Then, late one night about a week into their westward journey, they saw lights in a cluster ahead.

Again their hopes rose: *This time!* they thought. The twinkling lights resembled a beach-side town shimmering in the ocean haze. They counted the white lights—about 40 of them—as they slowly approached, and here and there among the lights were also a few red and green ones. The lights seemed to be moving, however, constantly changing position. Suddenly it dawned on them: the lights were not a village but fishing boats, probably congregating over a shoal of fish. It soon became apparent that the boats were small, so they could assume that nearby was a factory ship that took the catch on board and processed or stored it. It would be large and have the facilities to help them—medicines, perhaps a doctor, food, radio . . .

It was time to use the motor. They'd run it occasionally to ensure that it would continue to start when they needed it. Someone pumped the fuel line to prime the carburetor, then Donald choked the motor and pulled the starter rope. *Rescue, here we come!* he thought.

The motor coughed a couple of times. "Come on! Come on!" the men encouraged Donald. *"Pull 'em strong tri!"* The motor spluttered and spewed blue smoke, but continued to fire. Donald eased in the choke, careful not to flood the motor. As its pitch steadied, then increased, the men laughed and slapped each other. "Go, man!" they called to Donald as, under way at last, they turned off-wind and headed toward the lights.

They'd not motored for long when they began to realize that the lights weren't getting closer. In fact, if they were honest, the lights were now even further away than when they'd started the motor. The white lights of a fishing boat are attached high up on the mast. They tell other boats that they are working and also light the decks. The red and green navigation lights are usually much lower down on each side of the bridge. Eventually all they could see were the white lights and realized that the fleet had always been further away than they'd thought. Since they had little fuel left, they killed the motor and sat back once again, frustrated. But now, after yet another near miss, they began to think differently.

"No one is going to save us," Vince said in the darkness of the night. "We must plan to save ourselves."

"How do you mean?" Titus asked. "What can we do?"

"I've been thinking about this for some days now. I think the problem is not what we've done or not done, but what we *are*."

The other men reflected on his comment for a short time, afraid to answer. "God wants us to be different," Vince continued. "This might mean some changes in our thinking—in our hearts—as well as in what we do. We'll talk about it in the morning." The men mumbled an acknowledgment, knowing that there were things in their lives that weren't right—the missing money, their addictions to betel nut and tobacco. *Are we running from God, like the biblical Jonah? Do we have some sin in our lives? Was that the reason God seemed either unable or unwilling to answer our prayers? If we had already made right the wrong things in our lives, would we all be now sipping hot cocoa aboard one of the boats whose lights are just now disappearing over the horizon?*

Yes, tomorrow they would make things right. Having resigned themselves to changing their relationship with God, one by one they shut their eyes and went back to sleep. With the rising of the sun, they would get rid of the ways and things that were bringing trouble on them. Each one of them would establish a lifestyle that would see them through, no matter how long it took. They would appoint a new Captain—not of their boat, but of their lives.

CHAPTER
5

TAKING STOCK

Both for the men adrift and for their families at home on dry land, their respective situations in regard to food and water deteriorated with each day. The drifters were now completely out of food and water and were beginning to suffer exposure and dehydration. On Emirau their families suffered similarly as the drought worsened. They'd had no rain for months and the streams were mere trickles, wells and springs just muddy soaks, and the rainwater tanks were totally empty. In both places people looked to the heavens for relief.

The men's attempts to ration their food had been thwarted. What they'd thought would last them for months had already vanished. They'd had to eat it before it rotted in the warmth and constant damp. First of all they had experienced a glut as it ripened, then a famine. During the storms they'd lost some overboard, and what remained of the huge bunches of bananas had rapidly deteriorated. It was ironic. Now they were starving after having had to throw food overboard.

The only fluids they'd had was that in the food. They had no coconuts and had been unable to collect any of the rain that fell during the storms. Not surprisingly, when they weren't actually talking about food or water, they were thinking about it. Even when they slept they would dream about food and coconuts.

To supplement the small amount of fluid from their food, the men had begun to sip tiny quantities of sea water, gradually getting used to the taste and allowing their dehydrating bodies to adjust to the high-salt intake. Drinking salt water was easier, they discovered, if you heated it—as you would prepare a cup of tea. The salt water had an immediate physiological effect. First their limbs and joints began to swell and become painful. One surprising side effect was a total shutdown of their kidneys. For the rest of their days adrift none of them passed water. Their bodies had recognized their peril before their brains did, and had switched to a survival mode.

Depending upon climate and level of physical activity, the daily intake of fresh water should be somewhere between 10-12 eight-ounce glasses per day. Humans can survive without food for weeks, but without water they perish after a few days. Among the many health problems caused by not drinking enough fresh water are poor muscle and skin tone, muscle atrophy, joint soreness, muscle aches following any exertion, increased toxicity in the body, kidney stones, and, perhaps surprisingly, fluid retention and obesity.

To heat water they lit a small fire on a piece of heavy plywood, which sat on an upturned plastic crate. For fuel they tore strips of material from their clothing and shredded their rubber sandals. They had no matches, so they ignited it by unscrewing the sparkplug from the motor, then with a couple of pulls on the starter rope created a spark and, in a flash, the fire was burning. The addition of a small amount of gasoline helped to ignite it, and a dash of two-stroke oil kept it burning. They had a great little fire!

After five weeks at sea and the prospect of reaching China somewhat remote, their situation began to sink in, so Vince took on the responsibility of organizing them for survival. He set watches and rotations of their few duties—lookout, cooking, fishing, and steering. They decided to make a detailed inventory of everything they had. In their situation, everything—even things that appeared totally useless—might have some unrealized value or use.

In addition to the two oars tied to the boat sides for masts, they had two more which, if they saw land, they would use. The sail itself was about six by nine feet and bright orange. It was ideal as a square sail, but also as a beacon to any sharp-eyed lookout on a passing boat. However, it would only carry them ahead of the wind. Again and again they tried different configurations that might allow them to tack or at least move across the wind. But their efforts were useless.

They had several lengths of light rope, some of which they'd used to string the floats into a safety girdle, some heavy fishing line, and one medium-sized hook. In addition, they had the near-empty fuel tank. Since their two-stroke motor required oil to be mixed with the gasoline, they also carried a small plastic container of two-stroke motor oil. They'd planned to mix this with petrol for their return journey to Emirau. In a bag they found some large building nails. They could be handy, especially as they also had a sharpening file for the two axes on board.

Their only safety equipment was two flares. Even when expended, the heavy casings might have some residual use. They also possessed a flashlight, but it had no batteries. If they had some it would have made a great signaling device. Without them it was useless, and they were tempted to throw it overboard as they'd done with their radio when its batteries had died. Later they were glad they hadn't thrown it away, as it proved to be one of their most valuable possessions.

The castaways had no shortage of plastic net floats. Cut in half, they made cups for drinking, for storage, and served as fuel for the fire. They found many more floats during their voyage.

In addition, they were fortunate to possess two small Bibles that provided them with some intellectual and spiritual stimulation. They also kept a small diary-like book. In it they wrote a description of each of their days—the weather conditions, wind direction, their estimated position, the number and type of fish caught, and any sightings. It served as a kind of ship's log. From somewhere one of the men produced a small election poster left over from the recent national elections. The paper objects they kept dry in one of the watertight drums they also had on board.

But perhaps as important as what they possessed was what they didn't have: they had no matches, no pocket or bush knives, no mirror for signaling, only limited fishing gear, and no safety equipment such as life-jackets or extra flares. Any one of those things could have made the boat more comfortable, their lives less tenuous, and rescue more likely.

As the men took stock of their meager possessions, they had little idea of what all they would do with them during the coming weeks. Necessity and perhaps some divine prompting helped the men to find creative uses for the objects.

The six drifters thought about home a lot, wondering how their families were dealing with their loss. Six men missing—two from the same family—in the small Emirau community would cause widespread sorrow. But the men gave each other no hint of their creeping melancholy or depression.

Vince Benny was determined that he would somehow bring them back to land. He knew he had to keep up their spirits. Yet at the same time he thought about the kind of lives that some of the others had been living, and how they had abandoned their Christian heritage. And while he couldn't think of anything in his own life that had contributed to their situation, he wasn't so sure about the others. Constantly he prayed for them.

～

On Emirau the various families continued to pray for their lost *wantoks*. They were confident that with God the men could survive. They knew that Vince, being cool-headed and spiritually minded, would most likely become their leader. His faith, they hoped, would invigorate the small faith of the other less spiritual men.

A short time after the authorities had called off the search, another tragic event distracted the people on Emirau from the loss of the men. They might well be alive, but on Emirau the people were just about to bury the dead. A crocodile had seized a boy fishing among the mangroves and had eaten him. Not much remained for them to bury. This coincidence of a second tragedy also got the islanders to thinking.

All Pacific islanders are thoughtful, spiritual people with a well-developed consciousness. One thing that Western civilization and Christianity hadn't removed from them was their sense of portent. With their minds largely uncorrupted by movies, television and video, they are open to communication with the supernatural. They know that spirits—both good and evil—are real; that God's angels do His bidding; that He speaks to His people through dreams just as He did in Bible times; and that an evil devil constantly assails good, seeking to corrupt and destroy. With roots in a superstitious and relatively recent past, they observe the workings of providence and follow its dictates.

The tragedy of the crocodile attack in the mangrove, coming in addition to the loss at sea, gave the islanders pause. Just as on the boat the men were asking "why?" so on Emirau they began to do likewise. They wondered if the island's calamities—drought and famine included—indicated that God was withdrawing His protection from them.

As Christians they knew they should live a life of service, putting the wishes of others ahead of their own and living in peace with their fellow human beings. But during the past few months that had not been the case. Rather than Christian charity as a way of living, self-interest had been determining their behavior and relationships. On Emirau, as it has in most places, economic development ran headlong into a conservationist brick wall, and political conflict had arisen.

Some land-holders and those pushing to establish a new fish-processing plant on Emirau were at odds with other land-holders opposed to it. The conflict had reached the point to which it had divided the community, with those who supported development alienated from those who wanted to retain the lifestyle of the past. Animosities grew to the point at which harsh feelings were making former friends—even *wantoks*—into rivals and enemies.

Are these tragedies God's way of telling us, "Enough"? they wondered.

Some thought so. For others it was purely coincidence: bad things just happen. And aggravating their despair was the terrible drought. No one could remember a wet season that arid. Just as the men on the boat were discovering, the rain wasn't falling where needed. Usually the region had too much. Now there was hardly enough water for drinking and cooking, let alone washing or watering gardens. And while aid agencies were providing food for short-term relief they couldn't help with the water supply. People had to find their own water.

On Emirau people did their best to cope. The island is virtually all coral, with a very porous substrata below a shallow topsoil. Any rainfall or spring-fed stream quickly disappeared beneath the soil. Under the direction of community leaders and development experts, some of the wells sunk by the American Army in 1943-1945 were emptied of rubbish and deepened, but as they were not well positioned, they produced very little.

Incredibly the most reliable source of fresh water was beneath the ocean waves. The waves would wash up the sandy slopes, but bit by bit would fall lower and lower below the high-tide mark. Day or night the villagers would make their way to the beach with spades, buckets, and empty water containers. As the tide fell they dug deep holes into the sand, which filled like soaks with freshwater flowing from inland aquifers into the sea. They scooped up the brackish water in their containers and then carried it back to their houses and gardens. The water was sufficiently untainted to be drinkable, and certainly fresh enough for cooking purposes.

CHAPTER
6

EAST BY SOUTHEAST

The night eventually passed and morning brought the comfort of daylight. The cold disappointment of the missed opportunity in the night melted in the warmth of the rising sun. It was time to sort out a few things that they should have worked through long before. As soon as everyone was awake, Vince took up where he'd left off during the night.

"OK, brothers, listen up!" he commanded in quiet, firm tones. "We have had many near misses. This has been disappointing, but we are still alive. God could have saved us on any and each of those occasions if He had wanted to. But He didn't. What does this mean?

"I am thinking that perhaps God has some plans for us we do not understand, otherwise we might already be dead. But His plan is not to save us—at least not yet. So we must organize ourselves and prepare for a still longer journey. God is with us, and *He* will save us. Obviously He doesn't want someone else to or He would have allowed them to do so already. I think He has some things to teach us, like when Israel was wandering in the desert. We are in His hands. But I feel that there are also some things that we must do for ourselves—to allow Him to help us.

"First, we must put away from our lives and thinking everything that would prevent Him or His guardian angels from feeling comfortable with us on this boat.

"Joses," he said, turning to the big fellow, "do you think He could be with us while you chew your betel nut. You know what it does to your brain—it's just like beer. How can you believe God can speak to your mind when it is hyped up on the nut?"

Joses dropped his head, reluctantly nodding in agreement.

"And Cleveland. You have even admitted to being party to taking church money. While you owned up, you didn't tell where the money was or promise to return it. Maybe you didn't keep it yourself, but that was God's money, and you were involved. Do you wish to die out here knowing you robbed God?

"And right in our midst we carry tobacco. You know that our church teaches us that you should not smoke or drink, as these things affect the health of the brain and also the body. You know that your bodies are the temple of God, yet you continue to smoke. Will God help a hypocrite?

"I challenge you all to put these bad ways aside so that Jesus Christ can be the Captain of our boat. We may yet die out here, and, if we do, we must be ready for it, having our hearts open to God and our consciences clear. And, if like Jonah you've been running away from God, then now is the time to stop, or it may be necessary for God to see you cast into the ocean, too, so He can bring the rest of us to safety?"

Pausing, he looked at the other men, one by one. "So what do you say?"

In response to Vince's challenge the men discussed their ungodly lives and thought about past misdemeanors. They considered their future, which at this point looked fairly bleak, and, quite possibly, short. The thoughts Vince had expressed had been in their own minds. Here was a chance to get their lives right. They had nothing more to lose and everything, including life itself, to gain. Together they agreed to start over, this time taking God on board and dumping overboard some of the things that hindered Him. First went the tobacco, its owner realizing a certain incompatibility between his smoking and his pact with God. They tossed the remaining betel nut overboard, and it soon fell behind in their feeble wake and disappeared from sight.

Cleveland, whose problems were more than physical, didn't say much, but he gave some thought to Vince's words. His real problem was the guilt he carried but was now unable to make right. It seemed to worry him, and on a number of occasions he let small things slip that indicated his concern. He wasn't the most robust of lads, and his depressed mental state seemed to take a physical toll. He began to hint at what was going on inside his head, saying that he felt he would be the first of the six "to go."

The men also agreed to be a little more respectful of their God-Creator. Their commitment to prayer and worship to date had been haphazard and half-hearted. Now they drew up a roster for worships for which each in turn took responsibility, preparing a devotional thought based on the Bible. They'd grown up doing it, so it wasn't difficult to resurrect the old habit. Their worship would usually consist of prayer, a Bible reading, some discussion, and a song or two. Immediately beginning their schedule of morning and evening worship, they never failed in their commitment from that day forward.

The worships also included what they called "opening Sabbath" at sunset Friday evening; a Saturday morning "Sabbath" devotional; and "closing Sabbath" at sunset Saturday evening. They took extra time in preparing and participating in these three.

Besides their commitment to a spiritual life, they also organized themselves better in the daily, practical aspects of life. They set a watch that included keeping someone in the bow at all times to look out for a coconut or distant boat. Also someone stayed on the tiller, one fished, and another cooked. Each took their turn at the various tasks.

The Sabbath arrived with the sinking of the sun below the western horizon. The men had their first opening of the Sabbath worship, then settled down to sleep. It was their fifth week adrift.

The next morning, not long after concluding the first of their church-style worships, off their bow Titus spotted a floating object. It was that longed-for, prayed-for, dreamt-about coconut! Quickly Titus stripped, and following his friends' directions, swam and retrieved it. He swam water polo-style, bumping the coconut with his chest, back to the boat, which by now had drifted past him a little downwind.

He reached the boat and hung in the water, clinging to the lifeline strung around the waist of the vessel, caught his breath, then slung the nut inboard. With whoops of joy the others lifted the prize high. Grosby shook it next to his ear. "It is an old one, but it still contains milk!" he cried excitedly. "Let's party, everyone!"

Using an axe and the ferrule end of the file, they gouged a hole in the precious piece of flotsam, then, after a word of thanks to God, smiling and laughing they passed it from one to the next, each sipping his share.

"It's bitter, but, oh, it is sweet!" Donald exclaimed, smiling.

It wasn't the fresh sweet kulau they craved, but it was nevertheless palatable and refreshing.

"It is a blessing from God," Vince said. "He once brought water from out of a rock for the children of Israel when they were thirsty. Now He has done this similarly for us." The others agreed with his analogy. With a regular supply of coconut milk, they knew they could make it, even if they traveled 10,000 miles. As it turned out, God placed very few coconuts in their path, choosing to provide for them in other ways.

The coconut flesh was the first food they'd eaten for many days. It wasn't much when divided six ways, but it was enough for the moment and, obviously, was better than the alternative. Their lack of food was starting to show as their bones protruded through their skin and their dark eyes retreated deeper into their skulls. They needed more food, but from where?

The castaways would have to do more to ensure their survival. If they were to make it, then they could

THE JOURNEY

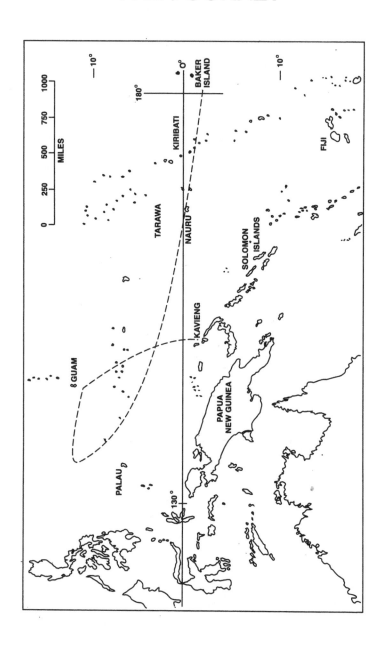

Crew members of the MV Evelina DaRosa *gaze across the Pacific, with a sister ship just astern.*

Vince Benny (left) and Titus Lauvus, on the grounds of the Tarawa Hospital, Kiribati.

*Drifters (L-R) Vince Benny, Joses Kareke, and Grosby Ume
pay their respects to former companion Cleveland Lauvus,
graveside, Bikenibau, Kiribati.*

*Drifters Titus Lauvus, Grosby Ume, and Vince Benny sit in the 19-foot
"banana" boat in which they wandered the western Pacific Ocean, in
tranquil Kavieng Harbor, PNG, following their return.*

The actual dinghy in which six Emirau Islanders sailed more than 4,000 miles, surviving with little food or fresh water for more than 84 days.

Vince Benny, who led the drifters in both their spiritual and literal journey halfway across the Pacific.

*Derrol Maisi, from Emirau Island, who organized
the drifters' homecoming celebration.*

*Carlos Barrata, who first sighted the drifters near Baker Island,
aboard the MV Evelina DaRosa.*

Kavieng Harbour, New Ireland province, PNG, from where the men left to begin their long journey across the western Pacific.

The five survivors at Jacksons Airport, Port Moresby, after flying home from Kiribati. (Photo courtesy Port Moresby's Post Courier)

Tools Used

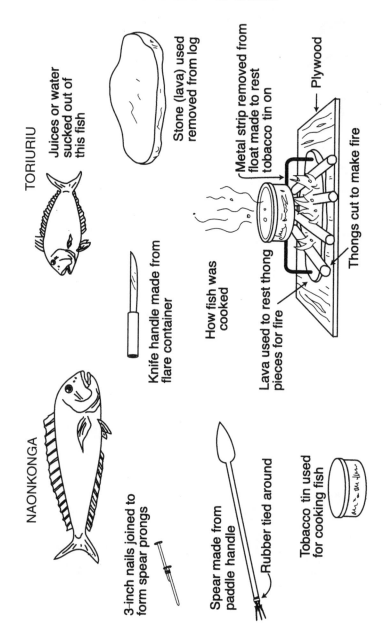

TORIURIU

Juices or water sucked out of this fish

Stone (lava) used removed from log

Metal strip removed from float made to rest tobacco tin on

Plywood

Knife handle made from flare container

How fish was cooked

Lava used to rest thong pieces for fire

Thongs cut to make fire

NAONKONGA

3-inch nails joined to form spear prongs

Spear made from paddle handle

Rubber tied around

Tobacco tin used for cooking fish

not rely entirely upon providence and luck. God had given each of them a good brain, initiative, and creativity. Alone, with plenty of time to think and work at ideas that might supply their two main needs of water and food, they decided it was time for a little creativity and industry on their part.

The wind, which had blown so consistently first from the south and then the east, had now stopped. They had either entered the doldrums where there was no wind, or they were at the change of season when the monsoon winds reversed, first blowing southeast out of Asia, then due south across the islands of Southeast Asia, into Australia. For days they sat becalmed, drifting westward on the current at perhaps 20 or 30 miles a day toward the minuscule islands of Palau and Yap in the western Carolines.

On the Monday following their first Sabbath worship, after weeks of vainly trying dozens of different lures, they finally caught a fish. Delighted, they lifted it carefully over the gunwales. One of them had a knife he'd fashioned from a piece of an aluminum float and the empty plastic tube from an expended flare. With a bit of filing it had sharpened nicely. Being aluminum, it was never that strong, but at least it was easy to put an edge on—and it didn't rust. They sliced a strip of rubber from a sandal, tore a few threads from someone's trousers, added a few drops of oil and petrol to it, then, with a spark from the motor, *"Em nau! Pairap* (Wow! Fire at last.)"

They placed the fish into the recently emptied tobacco tin and cooked the fish whole. One strip of rubber, they discovered, was enough to cook a fish to satisfaction—for a hungry castaway, that is. The fish, divided into six, wasn't much, but it was real food, and they were satisfied. In fact, it was best they didn't eat too much meat after starving for so long, or it might have made them sick.

As the food filled the stomachs, it also lifted their spirits and helped their good humor to return, but it was obvious that the line fishing was not going to provide enough food. They began to think about what else they might do. They looked through their meager inventory to see what useful items it might contain. Their supplies included the two spare oars, for which they had no real use (at least not until they neared an island), the nails (which were beginning to rust); and a file. In the now still ocean they could see fish swimming just beneath the surface, investigating the hull of their boat. *Why not fashion a spear?* It was something every kid on Emirau made and played with every day. *Why haven't we thought of it before?*

The men sharpened and barbed three or four nails using the file, then attached them to the paddle handle. Joses the plumber and handyman took no time at all to fashion a makeshift spear. Then, leaning over the side of the boat, his arm raised behind him, Joses watched until a larger fish came in for a nibble on the weed-infested hull. He lunged—and missed. But after trying a few more times, he eventually made a hit. Yelping with delight, he lifted a small, flapping fish on the end of the spear. It flicked itself from the spear and thrashed about in the shallow water in the bottom of the boat.

"Here is dinner!" Joses announced, his face beaming.

Again the starving men cooked and ate the fish. With a newfound, more reliable method of catching fish, the men felt more optimistic about surviving. By using their initiative and creativity they had managed to secure a regular food source that was satisfying, but somehow they needed to get more fluids.

After almost six weeks of drifting, the boat's hull below the waterline had become covered with a green weed. It attracted numerous fish, especially at night. The men would light an oiled piece of clothing and hang it over the side of the boat like a lantern, attracting the fish to the surface. It was easy to spear them like this, and they caught plenty during the coming weeks.

As a food source, the fish were excellent, but there was something more about these particular fish, called *toriuriu* around PNG, that the drifters hadn't realized. Because they were quite small, the men cooked them whole, not bothering to gut them. When overcooked, the flesh and innards gave up quite a lot of moisture, turning the dish into what the men generously termed "soup." The gut would completely break down into a nourishing "juice." They would simply suck it out of the crusty fish carcass in much the same way as one might suck the juice from a whole orange, leaving the flesh inside!

What made the *toriuriu* soup really special, however, was that the juice lacked the saltiness of other fish and was relatively "fresh," so was quite palatable as well as thirst-quenching. They caught scores of *toriuriu*—so many that they kept them in a bag suspended over the side of the boat in the splashing, cooling water. While fish kept the six alive, a little later it caused them their biggest scare during their time at sea.

Also, at night seabirds would rest on the gunwales of the boat as the men lay still inside. When the birds fell asleep, a stealthy hand would rise and grasp the unsuspecting prey, then break its neck. In the morning they would cook it, drain it of fluids, which they would drink, and then eat the flesh. And using its entrails as bait, they would attract more fish to the boat, which they hooked or speared.

Two days after catching their first fish their luck continued. A large log floated across their bow, and with an effort they paddled across to investigate. At a distance it looked as if it the barnacle-encrusted tree root did not have much to offer. But necessity suggested that they check to see if it might contain something useful. And it did.

Wedged between its roots was a dinner plate-sized flat stone. They wrestled the log against the side of the boat and, using their axe, broke away the rotting roots. The rock came loose and they took it aboard. It was an ideal replacement for their burnt-out piece of wood laminate that had been their fireplace until then. Now they set the flat rock on the plastic crate. On top of the rock they made their fire inside a metal frame, and on top of the frame set the tobacco-tin frypan into which went the catch of the day.

Many times they mentioned to each other how their change of fortune had coincided with their change in attitude and determination to accept God back into their lives. Although they still drifted helplessly, they could see His hand at work. Each morning and evening they thanked Him for His intervention.

CHAPTER 7

NECESSITY AND INVENTION

"*Ensin i bagarap; i dai pinis!* (The motor, it's dead)," Donald finally announced after pulling the starter rope for the hundredth time. "Salt water has corroded the coil or rusted the contacts. There's nothing I can do to fix it."

They were still catching plenty of fish, but they had to cook them in order to distill the vital life-giving fluid. They needed that motor—or at least the spark—but now it was of no use, except as a rudder.

But they didn't give up. Like all men with a small motor that won't start, they tinkered with it for days, trying to produce that elusive spark. They cleaned and prodded, disconnected and reconnected, scraped and filed—did everything imaginable—but still nothing worked. Then they ate dried fish, which wasn't so bad, but within a day or two their thirst returned as they missed the nourishment of the fish soup.

Next they tried different ways of sparking the petrol-soaked rag for their fire. Everyone had an idea, but none worked. For example, they placed the rag on the rock, then tried chipping at the rock with the axe, flint-like, hoping for a spark. Another time they rubbed pieces of plywood together to generate friction and heat after the fashion of the American Indians and Aborigines. And, of course, they tried the motor again and again. Nothing worked. Their failures left them worried, frustrated, and thirsty.

Joses, who had earned his living as a handyman, was more practical-minded than the others. Having experience in many types of work, he'd also learned to improvise. After yet another failed idea at lighting the fire, he sat in the stern of the boat, the hot sun above him, contemplating the problem. He glanced at his friends half asleep along each side of the boat, then stared at the pieces of oil-soaked rag and rubber heaped on the rock. The sun was terribly hot. As he thought about the fish they'd been eating raw for the past week and how nice it would be to get some of that warm soup into himself, suddenly an idea leapt into his consciousness.

"Hey, Donald," he called to his companion. "Take the tiller, man! I want to try something with this fire." Donald did as he was asked as Joses moved forward to the makeshift fireplace.

"Pass me the flashlight from inside the plastic barrel, Vince. I think our prayers for a fire might be answered."

Vince found the batteryless, useless flashlight and handed it to Joses, who squatted over the cold fire. Carefully he began to dismantle the torch. If there'd been batteries in it, it might have saved them two months before. In their dismay and frustration they'd been tempted to jettison it as they had the radio. Now he was thankful they hadn't. He looked back over his bony, brown shoulder at the sun. It had been their enemy. Now, he wondered, could he make it an ally?

As the others watched, he removed the small bulb and then unscrewed the reflector behind it that focused the relatively weak glow into a stronger beam of light. Now he would apply the concept in reverse. He would use the reflector like a magnifying glass to concentrate the heat and, hopefully, ignite a fire.

Joses worked away, trying a few different configurations of reflector and fuel. Soon a wisp of smoke rose from the oil- and petrol-soaked rags, then, fanned by the hot breeze, it suddenly burst into flame.

"Em nau! Em nau!" they exclaimed, slapping Joses on the back and punching him all at once. Joses beamed at his fire. They carefully fed pieces of rubber sandal to the fledgling flames. Quickly someone placed the tobacco tin on the fire with a freshly caught *toriuriu* in it. The fish cooked—and the cook, satisfied, went back to fishing!

The intense sunlight was fine for starting fires, but as it passed overhead day after day, they began to feel its effects. Despite their dark skins, they still suffered from sunburn and exposure, as they had little of their clothing left. Most of it they'd burned in their cooking. They were reduced to just trousers and soon—well, out here, who cared about modesty?—they would eventually burn them!

∽

The ability to improvise has always played a major part in surviving the kind of circumstances the men were now in. Scores of authenticated stories tell how people with very little in the way of resources, food, or fresh water outlasted months of deprivation. In almost every case, it seems, it's been their ability to think laterally that's made the difference. Every such experience contains episodes of hope, disappointment, and frustration. How one handles such disappointments as well as the possession of a disciplined courage—the stubborn determination to never give up hope—plus the ability to improvise, are the keys to survival.

One example is the 4,000-mile-long voyage of the infamous Lieutenant William Bligh of *Bounty* fame that began in April 1789 and ended six weeks later. Cast away in a 23-foot skiff with provisions for only a few days, he and 18 loyal crew sailed from near Tahiti to Timor in the East Indies (Indonesia). They accomplished the journey in a boat with less than a foot of freeboard because of his fine seamanship, resourcefulness, and force of personality. While it isn't easy to respect Bligh as a leader (the British colony of New South Wales mutinied against his harsh, petty, and dictatorial governorship in 1808), one must salute his effort in bringing to safety those under his command on the earlier occasion.

Another amazing aspect of his incredible voyage was that after an initial stop within the first few days, they completed it without encountering any other land. While the Pacific is littered with islands and atolls, it is a huge expanse of water with an insignificantly small proportion of land. It stretches 10,879.6 miles from the Panama Canal in the east to Mindanao in the Philippines in the west. Accounting for half of the world's water surface, the Pacific is half again as big as the Atlantic—and takes more than twice as long to cross.

The first Westerner to do so was the explorer Magellan. He entered the Pacific after rounding Cape Horn. His course took him through the heart of Polynesia, which includes hundreds of islands and atolls, and between Melanesia and Micronesia, further to the northwest. In those 12,000 miles he too never sighted land until he blundered into the Philippines. It should come as no surprise, then, that those who have the dubious honor of drifting the Pacific in a lifeboat only rarely make landfall on their own.

The famous U.S. car-racing champion and World War I fighter ace, Eddie Rickenbacker, also drifted across the central-western Pacific in a life raft not far from where the six Emirau Islanders were.

Although a civilian in October 1942, Rickenbacker went into the Pacific on a secret mission for the U.S. military. The B-17 on which he was a passenger aborted its take-off in Hawaii after locking a wheel. Then he and the rest of the flight crew finally took off from Hickam Field, Honolulu, in a borrowed plane and headed southwest. They had to ditch after losing their bearings and running out of fuel, the consequence of a malfunctioning radio-direction finder on their plane. With just enough time to evacuate the doomed aircraft after it pancaked, they had few items of any use with them when they climbed into the inflatable life rafts. And much of what they did possess, including flares, went to the bottom when their dinghy capsized in a storm a few days later.

Their fishing hooks soon rusted away and those that didn't sharks then bit off as they snatched the men's catch. The crew existed on an *average* of less than a cup of fresh water a day, but often they had none for days at a time. Being Caucasian, they all suffered intense sunburn. They also broke out in saltwater ulcers that created terrible discomfort and mental stress. The exposure and sickness led to hallucinations at times.

On one occasion when morale flagged and a soldier began to gripe, Rickenbacker, an obviously courageous and disciplined personality himself, berated his unfortunate traveling companion until the man pulled himself together.

Lieutenant James C. Whittaker, copilot of the lost plane, chronicled the story in his 1943 book *We Thought We Heard the Angels Sing.* He records one incident in which a crewman prayed that God would let him die and end his suffering. Rickenbacker, who professed no religion at all, was disgusted and leapt on him, ridiculing his lack of courage in an effort to lift him from his despair: "Cut that out!" he yelled. "If you want to pray, pray that the help that's coming will hurry and get here. Don't bother with that whining. God answers *men's* prayers, but not that stuff!" To a great extent it was Rickenbacker's willpower during the three weeks they spent as castaways that was responsible for getting seven of the eight men home alive.

In 1962 a group of Tongans en route to New Zealand were marooned on the South Minerva Reef for 102 days after a gale blew their cutter, the *Tuaikaepau*, onto it. The storm battered the hull to a few pieces of useless planking within hours. The group—which included a former and then current boxing champion of Tonga—had just a few hours to prepare themselves for survival before the tide, which flooded the reef entirely at high tide, turned and drowned them. They struggled across the coral and onto the hull of a marooned Japanese fishing wreck that lay on the reef on its beam ends.

They had neither food nor water, but they improvised fishing tackle and even managed to find a few items that allowed them to make fires and build a raft. As in the case of Lieutenant Whittaker and Rickenbacker, they survived because of the presence of a single strong character, David Fifita, the wrecked cutter's skipper, whom they accepted as leader. They were all men possessed of a strong religious faith and, like their Emirauan cousins, they held regular prayer meetings while marooned on the reef.

Using their ingenuity they cut mild steel from the hulk, which they fashioned into harpoons and hooks for fishing. Then they painted an SOS in huge letters on the upper side of the Japanese hulk to attract the attention of any plane that might pass overhead. In addition, they built a saltwater distillery efficient enough to provide each of them with a few ounces of fresh water a day; and they fashioned diving goggles for an attempt at recovering tools from the wreck of the *Tuaikaepau.*

They launched numerous drums, planks, and small rafts—even one carrying the bodies of their dead—into the ocean, each bearing the message of the their perilous situation and giving their position. Nobody found any of their messages. In the end they accomplished their own rescue by building a small outrigger (in fact, it weighed almost a ton), that carried three men—David Fifita, his son, and the *Tuaikaepau*'s carpenter—on a week-long voyage to the island of Kandavu.

And, as so often happens, even with rescue in sight, death snatches one final victim. In this instance a freak wave threw the outrigger onto the barrier reef surrounding Kandavu and capsized the vessel. The three, already exhausted by their ordeal, had to swim across the reef and lagoon to the shore. As Fifita Senior struggled through the water, he watched his flailing son drowning. Since the carpenter was also struggling, Fifita knew that if he went back to help his son, and the carpenter also failed to make it ashore, he would jeopardize the rescue of those remaining on South Minerva. He found himself forced to make a terrible decision. Although he would willingly have given his own life for his son, he swam on, reaching the shore but sacrificing his son's life. Eventually a flying-boat rescued 12 survivors from the reef.

One of the things that such survival stories teaches again and again is not to be discouraged when rescue seems so close but fails to materialize. The experience of Maurice and Maralyn Bailey illustrates this. They survived an incredible 119 days in a four-foot-six rubber dinghy after their yacht sank on March 4, 1973. *Seven* times ships passed them by at a distance of less than one-and-a-half miles. One of them actually stopped less than a mile away! Again, their ability to improvise and a positive, unflagging attitude enabled them to endure the four-and-a-half months adrift. Despite suffering from exposure, heat and cold, illness, hunger and thirst, storms, capsizing, damage to their raft, and loss of invaluable equipment, they maintained their fortitude and determination.

They had set out from the Hamble River in England during 1972, first crossing the Atlantic to Panama, then after negotiating the canal, headed west into the Pacific. Near the Galapagos a wounded whale holed their yacht. As their craft sank they snatched an assortment of items they thought could be useful. After weeks of boredom in their raft, to keep their sanity they fashioned a set of playing cards. They could only play on dry days when the cards weren't too soggy. When their morale fell, they sometimes found themselves verbally attacking each other, but then would immediately apologize. "I would rather serve a prison sentence," Maralyn said of her feelings at such times. "At least there would be a . . . date of release."

In this the Bailey's castaway experience was not unlike that of the six men. Like them, Maralyn kept a diary: "Every day becomes more of a nightmare," she once recorded. Along with her husband she survived for months in the middle of the world's largest body of water—and she couldn't even swim! Obviously, then, when you're adrift at sea, your strength as a swimmer isn't as important as mental stamina, a positive state of mind, and the determination to never, *ever* give up.

CHAPTER
8

COCONUTS AND A NEAR MISS

After almost two weeks of relative calm, the winds once again began to strengthen from the northwest as the monsoon reversed and swept toward the Southern Hemisphere. The seas began to steepen and dark clouds began rolling more purposefully across the graying sky. The drifters discussed the possibility of another gale, such as had nearly foundered their boat previously—and of their chances of surviving in their much more weakened state. After the clouds threatened for about a week without a real storm developing, the thought passed from their minds.

But it was still blowing quite strongly when, after weeks of fruitless searching, the lookout spotted a coconut bobbing about 50 yards to one side and not far ahead of their course. Immediately Titus dived into the water. He did not need to strip down—after all, he'd already burned most of his clothing—and swam strongly toward the precious object. The men were so desperate for a coconut that if you'd offered them a choice between one or an ocean pearl of the same size, they'd have looked at you in amazement. They had to have that coconut.

Titus's first strokes were strong, but weakened and stiff from weeks of inactivity, it was only with difficulty that he reached and retrieved the coconut and swam with it back to the boat. But it was worth it. The nut with its sweet milk was wonderful. And it was significant for more than just the physical nourishment and refreshment it provided. The coconut had drifted toward them, so an island must be lurking somewhere ahead. And being quite fresh with no signs of a long immersion, it indicated that it was probably not far away. Once again their hopes soared at the thought of making landfall.

But if there was land nearby, it would have to be directly in their track because of their maneuvering problem. And if they did come upon an island, they still faced immense danger as coral ringed most islands, either as a fringing or barrier reef. If they happened to make landfall during the night or in a gale or heavy seas, even a strong person might not survive being thrown onto sharp coral pounded by the sea.

On the seaward sides the coral rises almost vertically from the ocean floor thousands of feet below. Even a moderate swell throws up huge, steep waves along the outer side. Unless the timing, weather, sea, and tide were all favorable, reaching the island could be the most critical and dangerous part of their journey. But they still hoped for land, even with its potential for disaster.

But it wasn't a barrier reef that almost undid them. And it was another coconut, their third, that almost proved disastrous.

ADRIFT

As Titus's recent swim had revealed, they'd underestimated the impact of the lack of food and exercise on their bodies. Their bodies had obviously lost all excess fat, but more importantly, also physical condition. Cleveland's health had noticeably declined, and the others also continued to deteriorate.

The memory of that last drink of coconut milk was still fresh in their minds as a few days later they sat planning their eighth Sabbath at sea. They hadn't sighted any land since they had found the last coconut. Now it was almost sunset when someone spotted another green coconut drifting in the waves ahead. Although they pushed the tiller over as far as it would go and the boat headed closer toward the coconut, it was obvious that someone would still have to swim for it. Titus once again plunged overboard, swimming ahead of the boat as the others dropped the sail. The wind was fresh, and even without the sail it caught the little boat and continued to push it along.

Retrieving the coconut, Titus turned to swim to the boat, which by now was a little downwind from him. He swam hard, struggling to catch up, but seemed unable to close the small gap between himself and the drifting boat. The men began to worry.

"Swim, Titus, swim!" his friends yelled. "Come on, man. You can do it."

But as hard as he tried, encumbered by the coconut, he wasn't making up any distance. Instead of catching up, with each stroke he fell further behind. He began to disappear altogether into the wave troughs with his priceless possession. The wind whisked the boat along faster than he could swim.

Coconuts and a Near Miss

After the last time, he thought, *I should have known better.* But driven by the need for that vital coconut milk, his confidence had overridden his good sense. Titus couldn't understand where his strength had gone. It would normally have been an easy swim, but now, for the first time in his life, he began to picture himself drowning.

"*Rausim kulau! Rausim!*" Joses yelled, concerned at the perilous situation he could see developing. "Get rid of the coconut, Titus. Don't drown for a drink, man! Get rid of it. *Rausim, kwiktaim. Rausim!*"

Finally Titus let go of the coconut to face the more serious problem of reaching the dingy. He'd been struggling for almost half-an-hour and the boat was no closer. On the boat four of the men paddled furiously against the wind and chop while Cleveland stood poised with the length of rope in the bow, waiting to toss it to him. Titus knew that if something didn't happen in the next few minutes, he was going to die. His situation started to overwhelm him and his head dipped beneath the waves, his strength all but gone.

The men continued to call encouragement, praying as they paddled, but it was obvious that their friend could not make it, and with the rowers also tiring, they couldn't do much to help. The gap between them had increased to more than 100 yards and the men could only see Titus' head as he rose on an occasional wave. The others assigned Cleveland the task of spotting Titus' progress and reporting if he were still afloat or drowned.

All looked hopeless when suddenly Donald stopped rowing. The men looked at him, but from the look on his face they could tell something had occurred to him. They'd learned to trust his inventiveness.

"Stop rowing, all of you," he commanded. "I know what to do. Joses, Vince, grab the bailers and start to flood the boat. I will pull the draining plug. If we sink this boat, we can stop its drift. Titus will catch us then."

The dinghy still had the ring of floats attached about its waistline, so it was in no danger of completely sinking. Using cups made from plastic net floats they'd cut in half, the men scooped water and soon it began to rise around their ankles, then their calves. At last the wind lost its grip as the boat settled, then slowed and stopped altogether.

Titus could see that the boat was no longer moving away from him, and strengthened by new hope, he felt adrenalin rushing through him. *I'm not going to die—not after two months of surviving,* he said to himself, and gulping a couple deep breaths, put his head down and used the last of his strength to flounder toward the boat. The men in the boat lunged for him as soon as he came within reach, then held him alongside for a few moments as they all recovered their strength. Jubilantly they dragged the exhausted Titus into the boat. He tumbled into the half-filled hull and lay there panting, the water sloshing about him. He may have lost the coconut, but not his life.

As the six bailed the hull empty in the darkness, they discussed their near calamity. They agreed that because of their weakened condition no one would go overboard again—the risk was too high. No coconut, however enticing, was worth a life! As they once again opened the Sabbath that Friday night, they still petitioned God for a coconut. But they also thanked Him for the flash of inspiration that had saved Titus' life. *Perhaps,* they thought, *this is how it will be for us—rescued in the nick of time!*

They were a long way from home, but they believed that they were not alone. God was with them, guiding them toward some inevitable, invisible rendezvous, but they knew not where or when.

∼

Sabbath, Sunday, Monday, and Tuesday passed without further incident, except that behind them clouds formed and the seas continued to rise. They were used to the cycle of weather now—brilliant sunshine that scorched their dark, tanned skin, followed by a bit of cloud, then more brilliant sunshine. But nowhere any rain.

But if only it would. They had ample storage for water—the two five-gallon, screw-top drums and numerous floats that could hold gallons more, but the weather never broke, and no rain fell. They were at once victims of the climatic *El Niño* and yet were preserved, it seemed, because of the mercy of the heavenly *Niño.*

When dawn broke on the first Wednesday of their third month at sea, the castaways had their worship as always and assumed their assigned roles at the tiller, on watch, fishing, and in fire and food preparation. It was their routine. Grosby was the lookout in the bow. He stared ahead, always on the lookout for a coconut or another boat. Slowly he stood, and with one hand shaded his eyes from the glare and grasped the gunwales with the other. The others stopped what they were doing and followed his gaze.

"That looks like clouds around a mountain," he exclaimed, pointing toward the eastern horizon. "I think it might be an island."

The others looked hard, willing it to be so, but after so many disappointments reluctant to have their hopes dashed yet again. Along the horizon lingered some shapeless cottonwool cumulus clouds. The cloud they stared at was more gray and appeared to be anchored to the ocean. The way it was concentrated and billowed skyward suggested that Grosby was right. It was an island, probably about 15 miles away and just a few degrees off their course.

Although they didn't know it until later (they believed they were somewhere just off the north coast of New Guinea at this time), they were on a course headed for the tiny island of Nauru in Melanesia, well to the east of the Solomons and some 20 degrees (about 1,300 miles) east of their beginning point in Kavieng. Since picking up the nor'-wester, which carried them on a general course east-southeast, they'd probably traversed more than 1,800 miles. Added to the 900 they'd gone north from PNG in their first weeks adrift, and another 300-or-so to the west before picking up the monsoon, they'd probably journeyed more than 3,000 miles. Now, thankfully, they were just a few from its end.

Immediately they set about working the boat across the wind in order to run the island down later in the day. The boat turned a little side on to the wind, and began to move slightly across it. But mostly it continued to slip sideways, driven ahead of the wind in a direction that would take them somewhere north of the looming island.

For the rest of the day they watched the island grow larger, and they prayed intensely for landfall. They could see some detail of the island's topography by mid-afternoon, but were not close enough to see any signs of human activity. But with sunset just hours away, it became apparent the course to the island was too acute to their own to reach unless the wind miraculously shifted. Unless they paddled, they were not going to make it.

Dropping the sail, they broke out the paddles. But although they paddled until evening, it made little difference. Finally, with the island still well off to one side, the sun began to set. They made a sea anchor and tossed it overboard, hoping that the island might still be there in the morning. Soon night fell and nothing of the island was visible, and they floated on the dark and featureless ocean.

The night passed, but no one really slept. They peered into the darkness, hoping to see a fishing boat. As the gray of morning lifted, they peered toward where they hoped the island would be. It wasn't there. Stunned, they scanned the horizon. The currents and wind had carried them past the island and into the vast expanse of the Central Pacific. The island had vanished and along with it perhaps their best—their only—chance of rescue.

Depressed, the six slumped into the hull, each with his own thoughts. *Where is God?* they thought. *What does the future hold for us? Where will our journey end? Does someone have to die before we're rescued?*

CHAPTER
9

TRAVELING COMPANIONS

For some time two creatures—one overhead, the other in the deep below—had shadowed their vessel. As they wandered across the Pacific, the men saw many different forms of animal life. They observed flying fish, turtles, birds, and whales, but two species in particular attached themselves to the boat. The drifters had ignored them initially, but, when it eventually became clear they were not about to go away, their presence took on an ominous nature.

Birds wheeled and circled in the air above them every day. Sometimes they languidly drifted past on the heavy, humid atmosphere, or soared on a thermal before energetically diving into a shoal of fish. At times the men observed flocks of migrating birds beating hard into the wind, skimming the wave crests as they steered their course toward a rendezvous beyond the horizon.

If only we could be as certain of our destination, they thought as they watched the birds. The six knew that God cared for them as much as—even more than—He did for the common sparrow. They knew, when they saw the migrating birds, that God knew exactly where they were too, and He realized what their needs were.

Remembering back to the day they'd spent on Tench Island, before their misadventure began, they recalled that their drifter friend had told them that bird flight paths can indicate the direction of land. The castaways now studied the flight paths of the birds, hoping for some clue as to where land might be. But the birds flew every-which-way at any time of day. It seemed that advice was no use at all, so they discarded it. (It never occurred to them that they might in fact be in the midst of an island group—Kiribati—which, they were to discover later, was the case.) But what did it matter anyway? Their recent experience as they passed Nauru had proved that they couldn't alter course to a landfall even if they wanted to.

One especially large bird had refused to leave them since he'd first alighted on their boat more than a month before. Each night for weeks it stayed with them, sleeping just beyond their reach.

After spending each night on board, it would rise with the sun and wing out of sight into the distance. Late in the day it would drop from the clouds or glide low toward them just above the swell before settling like the mystical bird of Paul Gallico's story, The Snow Goose, on the gunwales of the boat. The men were amazed at how each evening it found its way back after spending the day out of sight. In the course of a day their position would sometimes change by more than 30 miles, yet it always located them.

The mystery bird never broke its routine. At first it

was something of a comfort, helping to break the monotony. They'd caught other birds that had presumed on their hospitality, but they couldn't bring themselves to kill this one, despite their hunger. For weeks it was merely a benign hitchhiker, along for the ride, but eventually, as time passed and they experienced further disappointments and their suffering intensified, they figured it was really some form of feathered bad omen.

The other creature that traveled with them was always more ominous. Its continued presence as a large dark patch in the water deep below their boat convinced them—if Titus's near-drowning hadn't—that they really needed to stay inside the boat. When the huge shark first came to the surface to investigate them, they estimated it to be somewhat longer than their 19-foot dingy. Since they could do nothing about it, they tolerated it, but its threatening presence always lurked in the back of their thoughts.

The *toriuriu* that congregated around the weed-covered hull were always plentiful, and catching them was easy. The drifters caught scores of them, sometimes a couple dozen in a day. The problem was how to keep them until needed. Sometimes they would gut and dry them. Another solution was to tie them in a hemp sack and suspend it half immersed from the boat's gunwales. As the water splashed onto the porous material and quickly evaporated, it acted like an air-conditioner, cooling the contents and preserving them just a little longer against the tropical heat.

One afternoon the men had eaten their fill of fish and placed the excess catch in the hemp bag and hung it over the side as usual. The top end of the bag was tied and hung just inside the boat's gunwales, where it made a slightly more comfortable headrest than the hard fiberglass for Joses, who lay with his back to the hull, head tilted skyward, eyes closed. Except for the lookout and helmsman, all the others lay half asleep.

Suddenly Titus's dark, suntanned skin went a shade paler as he stared wide-eyed at something behind Joses's shoulder.

"Joses! Joses! *Lukaut! Lukaut!* Watch out; behind you!" he yelled, his finger pointing at something just beyond the side of the boat.

Stirred from his daze, not sure of what the commotion was about and unaware of what was about to happen, Joses slowly began to lift himself upright. But he didn't move fast enough. As he began to lift his head from the sack, he felt something catch his unkempt, bushy hair. In the same instant, with Titus yelling at him to move, the bag jerked from beneath his head.

He swung around to see what had disturbed him and looked straight into the wide-open jaws of a leviathan. Rows of ugly white teeth, embedded in an iridescent pink mouth the size of a trash can, gnashed inches from his face as the huge shark gnawed at the bag of fish. Its head grabbed at the bag, thrashing left and right as it tried to drag it from the boat. The tail flailed the water into a lather as it attempted to gain purchase.

Instinctively Joses recoiled and twisted away from the threat, falling across the boat in a rush to put as much space between himself and the jagged teeth and foaming mouth. It was like the final scenes of the movie

Jaws, only this was the real thing. Joses lay against the side of the boat panting, his heart racing and mouth drier than usual.

For a few moments longer the shark thrashed the water and lunged at the side of the boat until it freed the bag and returned to the deep to consume it. The drifters stared at the water where the shark had been. The only evidence of their close encounter were a few innocuous bubbles bursting on the surface in their wake. The ocean leaves few evidences of its tragedies.

The attack by the shark became something of a metaphor for their situation. Like death, the shark's presence seemed always to be hovering off their stern. Death wasn't far away, they knew, and they had to be vigilant to keep it at bay. Yet they were all determined to survive, and, except for Cleveland, were confident that they would.

But from that night on, the words of the now familiar Shepherd's Psalm gained new meaning: "The Lord is my shepherd; I shall not want. . . . Yea, though I walk through the valley of the shadow of death, I will fear no evil: for thou art with me; thy rod and thy staff they comfort me . . ."

CHAPTER
10

DEATH KNOCKS

The near encounter with Nauru marked the end of two months at sea. Except for the storm more than a month before, they'd still not had rain. As the ever-present thirst, hunger, and discomfort weakened their bodies, despair crept into their minds. Their disappointment at failing to make landfall on Nauru ate away at their morale.

A week or so after they missed Nauru the sea and wind began to rise, and what looked like rain-filled storm clouds began to build. The wind made the ocean rougher, and they began to plan for another dunking. The men wondered if in their enfeebled state they could ride out a major storm. But for once they were pleasantly surprised, for although the wind and stormy conditions continued, it never threatened their boat.

And it rained!

Never mind that for three days they lay soaking wet, sleepless, and chilled in the damp hull. It was still glorious! They bathed in the life-saving liquid, quenching their pent-up thirst, filling themselves to bursting. Using their large plastic sail they quickly collected the rain and channeled it into the two five-gallon plastic containers that they'd been keeping for such a purpose. The men filled anything that would hold water, including fishing-net floats and those they'd cut in half for bailers.

As the boat itself began to fill with water, they attended to some housekeeping chores, swabbing the inside of the hull to flush away the build-up of salt. They washed everything, and by the time the rain finally stopped, they all felt stronger. The new water supply lifted their spirits. They hadn't been so happy since they'd left Kavieng, and it reinforced their expectation that they could—would—survive their ordeal.

But although they rationed the water, it still lasted only about two weeks. They drank the last of it about the same time as they drained the last drops of fire-lighting oil from its container. It was a double loss. Now they were unable to light a fire, unless conditions were perfect, so they ate raw, sun-dried fish most of the time. Their bodies soon missed the nourishing soup, and their hopes and health began to fade once more.

Then one morning they spotted a cargo boat loaded high with lumber and riding low in the water about two miles south of them. The boat was typical of the vessels that plied the coastal waters of PNG, and, recognizing this, Joses became convinced they were running parallel to the north coast of the New Guinea mainland where he'd intuitively—and incorrectly—assumed themselves to be. The boat failed to notice them, or if it did, simply assumed them to be fishermen from some local island and thus ignored them. It never deviated from its course and soon disappeared over the horizon.

But Joses was convinced of his dead-reckoning and argued with Vince that they should turn southward, sailing and paddling as best they could toward whatever land lay just over the horizon. But Vince remained unpersuaded, arguing that they should not deviate from their course following the wind. A short time later they spotted a large tethered float in the distance. Now things became heated. It was just like the ones anchored a few miles to seaward from Kavieng, Joses argued, so home was not far away, and they should go look.

All the evidence suggested to him that home was just to the south. Angrily he yelled at Vince, demanding that they at least try, but Vince remained unmoved.

In retrospect it appears that such signs of human activity indicated their proximity to the Kiribati group, but they were unaware of this. Kiribati, after all, consists of just a few square kilometers of low coral islands and is mostly empty ocean. So they kept on following the wind and the daily routines resumed. Vince also had pragmatic reasons for staying on their course.

When once before he'd caved in to their demands and changed course, they lost their food and water supply. On that occasion they'd steered away from the wind for three days and the *toriuriu* that followed their craft immediately deserted them. During that entire time they neither saw nor caught a single fish. Then, when eventually they resumed running with the wind, as if by magic the *toriuriu* returned. Vince felt that a guaranteed food supply was more important than vainly wandering the desert ocean looking for land that might not exist. He insisted that they continue their present course, and the brief mutiny eventually ended with no hard feelings.

But soon after this incident, probably due to the lack of cooked fish and fresh water, Cleveland's health began to rapidly deteriorate. No one knew for sure, but they suspected it was more than just his sipping too much salt water during the night. Grosby was most concerned and took it upon himself to see that Cleveland received the best of the food.

With Cleveland's life in jeopardy, they prayed with a new desperation for rescue. Then, when Donald's health also began to rapidly decline, they could see that without more fresh water they all would soon be dead. They looked and felt terrible, and were almost completely naked. The sun still burned them despite their naturally tanned skin and thick woolly hair. The men were in a pitiful and desperate state.

However, except for the two who were sick, they continued to function, keeping up their watches and tasks. One afternoon they hooked a very large fish. It trailed the line this way and that as they gently played it, using all their native skills to avoid losing their tackle. Eventually the fish tired and they pulled it close to the boat where they grabbed it with their hands and dragged it inboard. To their dismay they discovered they'd snagged a *naonakonga*—a small dolphin-like fish about three feet long.

It was the largest fish they'd caught, but that wasn't good news entirely. Island tradition said that to catch such a large fish in an unusual place was an omen that someone was about to die. But ignoring the belief, they ate what they could.

Within an hour each one of them came down with food poisoning. They rolled about the boat, clutching their stomachs, heaving and groaning in pain. They all felt so ill that they thought they would immediately die. Of course, they didn't, but the message seemed clear: someone soon would.

Cleveland's condition, perhaps aggravated by his energy-sapping bout with food poisoning, worsened further. Everyone knew, barring rescue, that he didn't have long to live. Even as they encouraged him, willing him to survive, his strength drained away to the point at which he could barely respond or move. His eyes sank into their sockets and his bones protruded through his skin. When a person starves, the body considers the fatty tissue around the eyes to be the most dispensable, so it's the first consumed.

Despite their intense prayers for Cleveland, they felt that his death was imminent. It occurred to them, although they avoided mentioning it, that their failure to be rescued was in some way connected to his presence in the boat.

Does he have to die before we can be rescued? they wondered. *Is Cleveland like some sort of Jonah of the Old Testament, who had to be thrown overboard to ensure the survival of the boat on which he sailed? Can it be that rescue is impossible until Cleveland has made his peace with God? Or will he—or another—have to die first?*

It seemed that Cleveland was having some of the same thoughts, for on the Friday morning of their twelfth week at sea he awoke and croaked, barely audible, through his parched lips, "I had a dream last night. And I don't think I'm going to make it. I am going to be the first to leave. Then, maybe, things will be right for you . . ." His voice trailed off.

Dreams are important to the Pacific islanders. Such an idea is strange to Westerners, whose minds are constantly bombarded with make-believe images and concepts, and who are usually taught not to take dreams seriously. Yet, for the Christian, the Bible offers examples of God speaking to people in such a manner. He used dreams and visions to communicate to Abraham, Jacob, Daniel, Joseph, the apostle Peter, and many others, including ordinary people.

The islanders, who see and accept the supernatural at work around them every day, had learned to interpret dreams. When Cleveland told his friends that he had dreamed he would soon die, they accepted that it would be so. It was a familiar concept.

In the culture of Emirau, for example, if someone dreams about a sick person, and a relative of the sick person is nearby, people consider it a warning of their death. Or if in the dream the sleeper sees a sick person covered by palm fronds or a blanket and the next day the dreamer finds them in that condition, this also indicates that their death is imminent.

And back on Emirau at this time many different people dreamed about Cleveland—the same dream, amazingly—and interpreted it as meaning that he was about to die. As word of the dreams reached his relatives it brought sadness, but it also had its positive corollary: If

DEATH KNOCKS

Cleveland was just now *about* to die, and as this was their first such dream about the men, then the other men were most likely still alive! Such an apparent confirmation of the lost drifters' survival brought a muted hope and reassurance to their families.

The Friday—the preparation day for the Sabbath—on which Cleveland made his announcement was like the previous 11 they'd spent drifting. The sun shone hot and the bright-blue sky faded as it fell toward the haze-filled horizon. Overhead gulls squawked, while at a distance other seabirds dived into the ocean, emerging with a silver, shimmering prize. A few fish broke the surface near the boat in the never-ending swells.

The men busied themselves with their duties as best they could, trying not to think too much about Cleveland. Vince sat close by his friend, comforting him and offering encouragement. Donald, also, was needing help, as he had also deteriorated. Suddenly Joses yelled. He had another big fish on the line. It jerked the line tight, first running away from the boat then back in and under it before turning away again.

"Hey, man. Em i bikpela pis! (It's a big fish.)" he called excitedly.

Finally the fish flagged, and laughing now, the others offered him advice on how to land it. They were glad for the interruption of their routine. This time it was a large tuna, which they knew they could safely eat. They decided to make a fire and cook it right then, and eat it for the Sabbath eve meal. They were now dispirited, almost past caring, and a good feed of fish steaks would help them feel better.

With what was almost the last of their clothing and using anything else flammable, they kindled a fire, then gutted and cooked the tuna. That evening, after they'd opened the Sabbath, the men enjoyed the best meal they had had in quite a while. Donald and Cleveland also ate, the fish being cooked and tender. In fact, it was so nice and so plentiful that they all overindulged, and their stomachs full, one by one they nodded off into deep sleep. They didn't bother to post a watch for the night. After all, it was the Sabbath—the day of rest—and they surely needed rest. And, perhaps, it would be the day they finally found it.

Vince slept in the stern, the others spread along each side, facing each other, their heads back and eyes shut. They slept solidly until about 3:00 a.m. when Joses suddenly awoke and sensed something wrong. He had been sleeping alongside Cleveland, who rested against him. Now, as he gently shifted Cleveland's weight away from himself, he realized that the other man didn't stir or move at all. His skin felt cold. Cleveland had finally died.

Joses looked into the dark night sky, the stars hidden behind some cloud, and offered a short, silent prayer, then called to the others.

"Cleveland—he is dead!" was all he could say.

The five men were quiet for a time as the reality—though long anticipated—sank in. They had become so close, being together for three months. They thought about Cleveland, his family, and their situation. Donald felt a twinge of guilt for his part as boat captain in bringing about the tragedy that finally led to Cleveland's death. Each of the men began to weep.

"Perhaps catching the *naonakonga* has brought us bad luck," a voice in the darkness proposed to no one in particular.

"I don't believe that is true. Cleveland knew it was coming. Before."

"What should we do with his body?" someone else asked. "How can we bury him at sea? I don't know. His body belongs on the land. Perhaps we should keep him with us for one or two more days—just in case we make it in the next day or two."

In the darkness, together, the others agreed.

"He had made his peace. I am sure of that," someone said.

"Maybe one of us had to die before the rest could be saved. You know—and I don't like to say it—now that Cleveland is dead, things might change."

In fact things had changed—dramatically so—and more than they realized as together they gently and respectfully wrapped Cleveland's body in a blanket. They sat in the darkness and talked until the sky began to lighten with the promise of dawn. It was about 5.30 a.m. when they began their morning worship.

It was a bit earlier than usual, but right then it was their only hope. They needed the strength that only prayer can bring. And as they prayed, their closed eyes trickling tears, the sun cast a shadow across them as it rose behind their orange sail ahead of them. There was no point in praying for Cleveland now—his judgment day had come. So they simply pleaded with God for a coconut or rain, or to sight a boat that it might rescue them.

OUT OF THE BLUE

After they had finished worship and decided to keep Cleveland's corpse on board for one day, the men went to their duties. Joses left the men in the stern where Titus lay weeping on the body of his *wantok* and crawled the few feet to the bow to take up his watch. He had to bend his head and shoulders low in order to clamber beneath the sail strung across the boat.

Dragging himself into a comfortable sitting position, he squinted into the silver flashes of sunlight bouncing off the gentle waves that washed languidly ahead of them before the light breeze.

"Em nau!" he exclaimed aloud, as he stood up, shocked and bewildered by what he saw. Dead ahead, about 150 yards away and blocking their path, was the shining blue hull of a massive ship! It made no bow wave and appeared to be stationary. Waiting. With the sun low and directly in their eyes, none of the five had seen it looming.

"It's a boat. It's a boat," he stammered. *"Yupela ilukim!"*

he called to his friends, who turned in stunned disbelief. "Vince, Donald, Titus, Grosby! Look, it's a boat."

Raising his arm, he weakly waved to the line of faces that peered down from behind the ship's railing, then slumped to the floor of the dinghy, tears coursing down his cheeks.

"Thank God, we're saved!" someone whispered.

～

Captain Larry DaRosa, 40, from San Diego, California, stared at the glowing face of the gyro compass in the darkened bridge of his fishing boat the MV *Evelina DaRosa*. Something was not right. At 4:00 that afternoon—he distinctly recalled doing so—he'd ordered his ship's course set to 205 degrees. In a little more than 24 hours they would rendezvous with the sister ships of the fleet, which were working another patch of ocean some 400 miles south-southwest of his position.

We'll miss the fleet by miles if we stay on this course, he thought to himself.

He continued to stare at the compass face. The needle hovered above 225 degrees, or due southwest—20 degrees west of his planned vector. Somehow the *Evelina*'s course had been altered, but by whom—or why—he had no idea.

Yes, he was clear in his recollection of the order he'd given to Joe, the *Evelina*'s navigator. Joe was a competent and trustworthy second-in-command who would never change a course without first consulting the captain or, at the very least, inform him as soon as possible afterward. Captain DaRosa, arms folded, stared ahead into the blackness that hid the *Evelina*'s bow, pondering the implications of the new course. He wondered if he should order the ship brought back to the heading he had ordered.

This really is strange, he thought. *Why would Joe set this course?* In his 25 years at sea, he'd never experienced anything like this. He paused for a few moments more, then walked to the chart table and stared at the map of the Western Pacific spread there. A pencil line and series of crosses revealed the *Evelina*'s movements during the past few days.

It's a safe enough course, but where will it take us? he pondered. *There must have been a misunderstanding.* Taking a deep breath, he scratched his head. With his finger he drew an imaginary line diagonally across the map, then stabbed at their likely position 24 hours hence.

Perhaps it will prove to be a lucky course, he mused and stepped back, his mind made up. *I'll leave it be. And wherever it takes us, the fishing has to be better.*

It had not been a profitable two weeks thus far on the voyage. The 230-foot high-tech trawler *Evelina DaRosa*—named in honor of his mother, a part owner—was considered to be a "lucky" ship. It's freezers could hold 1,100 tons of frozen tuna, and usually would have been close to that at this point. But this particular trip had begun slowly. The freezers were still nearer empty than full.

The *Evelina* was one of a fleet of fishing vessels based in Pago Pago, American Samoa, and usually fished as part of a fleet. But rather than stay with the fleet, this time Captain DaRosa had decided to go solo. It was not a good decision. He'd thought to try his luck much further east than was normal for October, but wherever he went the tuna were scarce.

Returning to the center of the bridge, he checked the ship's log. They were making 14 knots, a bit less than she was capable. With a shrug he walked from the bridge to his cabin nearby. He would ask Joe about the breach of orders in the morning. It wasn't urgent—just intriguing. Since it was after 10:00 p.m. and Joe would be asleep, Captain DaRosa decided not to bother him.

Once in his cabin he undressed and washed, then, as was his custom, knelt and offered a prayer, switched off the light, and slid into his bunk. He drifted off to sleep still thinking about the altered course.

Throughout the night the *Evelina* plowed southwest into a slight sea. Using her sophisticated sonar and fish-finding equipment, the crew continued the hunt for schools of fish. But even though the vessel was equipped with the latest in fishing gear—she even had a small helicopter for spotting—intuition and a knowledge of the sea and the ways of fish still came ahead of technology.

During the day the crew used binoculars to scan the ocean for surface activity that might indicate the presence of big fish below. For example, when they saw seagulls diving into the ocean, picking up small fish, that usually indicated deep-sea tuna below driving the smaller fish to the surface. Thus, beginning at first light that Saturday morning, from a position high on the *Evelina DaRosa*'s mast a lookout—a fish spotter or "mast man"—swept the horizon in search of telltale signs. Only the dogwatch crew were in bed (or needed to be) and most of the crew was busy with maintenance tasks or in preparing the long lines for when they spotted fish. The monochrome gray of the newborn day was beginning to dissolve in the gold of the rising sun when the mastman abruptly called a warning over the deck PA.

"Orange marker on the horizon, to starboard," it crackled to everyone, including Captain DaRosa who was already occupying the bridge.

As ocean-going fishing vessels plough their invisible furrows, they often spot large logs that have washed down flooded rivers and even large steel shipping containers that have fallen overboard from carriers during storms. Sometimes these will float almost out of sight just below the surface. Extremely dangerous to shipping, especially to smaller craft, they have holed many an unsuspecting cruising yacht and sunk a few commercial boats as well. To help prevent this, fishing boats sometimes attach floats with brightly colored flags to pieces of flotsam to warn other ships of the hazard. Sometimes they add radio trans-mitters, which they use to plot the ocean currents.

"OK, let's have a look," Captain DaRosa said to the helmsman. "Bring her around to 270 degrees. Due west, please. We'll see if it's a container. If we're lucky, there might be fish around it."

The *Evelina* heeled slightly as she turned to the right, the sun reddening the clouds directly astern. For 30 minutes they headed west into a low swell and light breeze, doing 15 knots. Little by little the orange object grew larger. It appeared to be moving toward them, as the gap between themselves and the object closed more rapidly than they expected.

When about five miles from the object, the mastman, Carlos Barratta, again called over the PA. "It's no good," he said, sounding a little disappointed. "It's just a small sailboat. No fish this morning, brothers!"

"Then let's get back on course for the fleet," Captain DaRosa told the helmsman. "Resume sou'-sou'-west." The helmsman spun the wheel and the *Evelina DaRosa* began a long turn southward.

But just as the ship began to heel to starboard, Captain DaRosa once again felt the unease of the night before. Thinking again of the altered course and now this object—this boat—he walked over to the chart table and unrolled a map.

Experience gained from 25 years at sea and intuition, inherited from his Portuguese father and grandfather—also fishermen—told him something definitely wasn't right.

It's odd, such a small craft fishing so far from land, he thought as he stared at the map spread before him. *We're more than 600 miles from the nearest inhabited island.*

Standing, he looked across his starboard beam, where the sun's rays were just now catching the orange sail atop an almost invisible hull.

"Bring her back due west!" he ordered the helmsman, who hesitated in disbelief. "Let's take a close look at that boat. Those guys are either a lot braver than I am, fishing way out here in that boat, or they're in a whole lot of trouble! Either way I want to find out." The surprised sailor obeyed, and spun the wheel.

Almost 10 minutes passed before Carlos the mastman called over the PA again. The orange blob, glowing now, was about three miles distant and dead ahead. The inquisitive crew began congregating on the bow when the PA blurted again.

"I see two, possibly three, men in an open boat," Carlos said. "The sail looks makeshift. Someone's standing, waving. Someone's hailing us. It's a mayday. I think they need assistance."

The *Evelina* continued to close for another 10 minutes, then, with the small boat only a couple of hundred yards away, slowed and turned hard left until it was beam-on to the drifting boat, waiting for it to float to them in the light following breeze.

From his position on the bridge Captain DaRosa ordered a rope ladder dropped over the side by the crew who lined the starboard railing, staring at the diminutive, weatherbeaten dinghy with its human cargo. In the dinghy's bow someone now stood up and lethargically waved before sitting down again. Other faces, gaunt, appeared from behind the square-set sail that had obscured them. They, too, waved. The *Evelina*'s crew waved back.

The dinghy soon traversed the final few yards, then bumped against the side of the *Evelina*. One of the crew threw a rope to the man in the bow of the craft, which swung on the breeze close to the side of the *Evelina*, then was still. Its long and dreadful voyage had ended.

Captain DaRosa leaned out over the bridge railing and looked down into the boat. Five pairs of sunken eyes stared back. He turned away, his eyes smarting.

"It was something I will remember for years to come," he confessed later. "These poor, emaciated men—too many for such a small boat—barely able to raise their arms to wave up at me. . . . Looking up at me, their eyes said it all. They'd been through a hell on earth that few could imagine."

As he gazed back, he realized that one of them was lying on top of a blanket covering what appeared to be another person. The head of the person was covered. The man lying on top of the blanket was wailing, obviously feeling some great sorrow despite his rescue.

"Is that man alive?" Captain DaRosa called down.

One of the men in the boat glanced up, understanding, but appeared hardly able to respond. He simply motioned a no and continued to gaze up at his rescuers.

As did the whole crew, Captain DaRosa felt great sorrow and pity for the men in the flimsy boat that now nudged the *Evelina*'s steel hull. Then, as he grasped the fact that the man beneath the blanket must have only recently died, a wave of self-recrimination swept over him.

If only I had gotten here sooner, he thought. *If I hadn't wasted time yesterday, I could have been here in time to save him.*

He looked again at the men in the dinghy who futilely tried to grasp the swinging rope ladder. "I'm sorry! I'm sorry!" was all he could say. "I'm sorry I was too late."

～

The conflicting emotions of Cleveland's death in the night and their rescue now was too much for the men. After standing for a few moments to gaze and wave at the boat, all they could do was sit in silence and stare at the ship ahead of them as their craft drifted across the last few yards to safety and rescue.

They bumped into the blue-painted hull of the rescue ship. A man tossed them a rope, which Joses securely fastened. Then they lay back, unable to help themselves, emotionally exhausted by the moment as well as 12 weeks of starvation and exposure to the elements. When they tried to grab at the rope ladder, they suddenly found themselves too weak to move.

Someone called to them from high in the ship's superstructure. *No, Cleveland isn't alive.* They could hear, but had no breath to reply.

Through brimming eyes they watched as a powerboat approached them from the stern. Big Samoan hands gently lifted them into it, then sped back to where a crane stretched out over the ship's side. The boat crew quickly attached lines hanging from the crane and with everyone still in the speedboat, they were winched the few feet to the deck. Then, like so many tuna in a net, the survivors, almost completely naked and hardly able to walk, tumbled out. They sat quietly, staring back at their amazed and curious audience.

Someone brought some water and they slaked their thirst, confident for the first time in three months that it was from a bottomless cup. After the five had recovered, the ship's crew helped them inside to the galley. They lay back on some soft mattresses, secure at last. God had answered their prayers.

Captain DaRosa made preparations to get the men to a hospital as rapidly as possible. All were in need of medical treatment, and the *Evelina* had no doctor. Its crew hauled aboard the 19-foot boat that had carried the six men more than 4,000 miles across the Pacific and lashed it to the deck. Then they stowed the few possessions. They wrapped Cleveland's body in the castaways' sheets of plastic and sealed it with tape before placing it in one of the boat's large cold-storage bins. In the galley the surviving five sipped drinks through blistered and swollen lips.

On the bridge Captain DaRosa notified the Coast Guard in Honolulu, Hawaii, and asked for advice on how to care for the survivors, then went below to see them. Again as he looked at them, emotion overcame him. "I'm sorry! I'm sorry!" he whispered. "I'm sorry I didn't come earlier. I could have saved you all."

CHAPTER
12

A COURSE FOR HOME

The *Evelina* turned northwest and quickly reached its maximum speed of 15 knots, heading for Tarawa, the main island of the Republic of Kiribati, where there was a hospital. The crew would not be fishing for a while.

Captain DaRosa tried a number of avenues to contact PNG authorities, each time without receiving a response. Eventually he reached Felix Panjuboe, director of the Forum Fishing Agency in Honiara, Solomon Islands. He gave a great deal of assistance and advice. Captain DaRosa also spoke with a doctor in Honolulu who advised him about caring for the dehydrated and starving survivors. The men were to have a limited fluid intake for the first six to 10 hours—anything more could be dangerous—then afterward all that they wanted. And the same went with food.

The captain's first reaction to the men's plight had been to offer them all the food they could eat. But now, to their chagrin, he regretfully informed them they would have to eat and drink cautiously. The news devastated them at first, but they accepted it, and settled down to imagine their first real meal in almost three months. But in the meantime, they didn't go without entirely. Some of the crew, feeling sorry for their starving guests, smuggled a few pieces of easily digestible cake to them when the captain wasn't about.

The survivors had no idea of where they were and the extent of their voyage. At first they pleaded with Captain DaRosa to take them directly to PNG. Because it was much closer, he insisted on Kiribati. But, he said, he might get to PNG sometime. About 4:00 Saturday afternoon Captain DaRosa radioed Kiribati, informing them he was headed their way. Honolulu would make all arrangements for their arrival, the authorities informed him.

He asked the men whom he should contact in PNG to tell them of their rescue. Like all large seagoing vessels, the *DaRosa*'s communication equipment included radio, fax, and satellite telephone, so it would be possible to contact anyone they liked as long as he had a telephone. But on Emirau there are none—just VHF radio, which was inaccessible from the *Evelina* thousands of miles away.

Between them the men couldn't recall the telephone number of even one Kavieng friend or relative. *How can we make contact?* they wondered. Then someone had a burst of inspiration. Among their few belongings was a piece of paper—an election poster promoting the "Hon. Ian Ling Stucky, MP, Member for Kavieng Open" as the New Ireland Province member in the National Parliament. They were sure that it had a telephone number on it. One of the men had picked it up for no apparent reason back in Kavieng and kept it. Now, like so many other seemingly useless bits and pieces they'd carried with them for 12 weeks, its purpose became apparent.

The flier included Ling Stucky's postal address, his telephone number in Kavieng, and a fax number at the parliament office in Port Moresby. Expectantly the men waited while Captain DaRosa phoned the number, but no one answered. Captain DaRosa tried a few more times, but always without success. Then it occurred to the men why no one was answering.

"I think that telephone number might be his business number," Vince suggested. "And as it is still Saturday afternoon in PNG, the business will be closed for the Sabbath." Vince tried to explain that although Ling Stucky was a member of parliament, government offices shut on Saturday and Sunday in PNG. Given the added difficulty of their limited English vocabulary, Captain DaRosa, found it hard to understand.

"It is like in the Bible days," Vince tried to explain, "when everyone observed the seventh day of the week as the Sabbath day of rest. Only now we have two days—Sunday and Saturday."

Eventually, with Joses' help, the captain drafted a fax, which he sent to Ling Stucky's office at the PNG Parliament in Port Moresby. There someone picked it up and within minutes relayed the good news of the men's rescue to Emergency Services in Kavieng, where it was late afternoon. The duty officer received the message and promptly radioed Derrol Maisi, a Ward Member (a position like a local government councillor) on Emirau.

A Course for Home

Within minutes of receiving the news on Emirau people began to congregate around the radio room. They could hardly believe that anyone could have survived so long at sea. But although everyone wanted to share the joy of the occasion, the mood was still somewhat somber, because they now knew for certain that one of the six men wouldn't be coming home.

But the news of the rescue wasn't totally unexpected. Earlier that day Vince's father, known as Benny, awoke early after being disturbed by a dream. He arose from his bed and began to prepare for the day. But he couldn't get the dream out of his mind. A short time later he met Derrol Maisi, a friend, and told him the dream.

"I was standing in the shadow of the palms, high on the beach of Emirau," he said, "when on the ocean I saw a small boat approaching. It came right to shore below where I stood and the waves pushed it onto the sand. Someone stepped from the boat and began to walk toward me, so I went to meet them.

"As I came closer, I recognized the man as my son, Vince. I rushed to him, extending my arms in welcome. But as I came close to him and was about to shake his hand, the man—Vince—he just disappeared! I think that very soon my son will be found—alive."

Given the two-hour time difference between the longitude of the *Evelina* at the time of the rescue and Emirau, it's conceivable that just as Vince and the others completed their worship at about 6:00 a.m. and looked up to see the *Evelina DaRosa* towering above them, Benny was waking from his dream on Emirau.

Even though Captain DaRosa didn't quite understand the beliefs of his Seventh-day Adventist guests, he was not ignorant about spiritual things. He had a deep faith of his own and trusted in God and His power. So when the men began to tell him of their experiences on the sea, their prayers for rescue and their faith in God, he understood. He knew why it was on that Saturday morning that he found himself straddling the invisible path of the drifting dinghy. As a believer in God, he realized that providence had led him to that featureless spot—just a couple numbers on a map—in the midst of the vast Pacific Ocean.

The day after their rescue, Joses and Vince—the others were still incapable of walking—went for a look over the ship. They found their way to the door of the bridge. Captain DaRosa invited them in. They were amazed at the technology—the radar and navigation equipment, sonar, depth sounders, radios, and telephones that filled the place. Captain DaRosa then took them to the map table and pointed to a spot marked on it.

"That's where I found you," he said pointing to a cross: "00° 16' S, 177° 30' W. The nearest land is Baker Island, an uninhabited atoll about 70 miles southwest of there."

The men were amazed. They looked at the mark and traced their journey to the edge of the map, where Papua New Guinea lay more than 2,000 miles to the west. They'd thought they were still somewhere in the vicinity of PNG! Captain DaRosa charted their probable course based on their sightings, the prevailing winds, and his estimate of their speed.

The captain guessed that on a number of occasions land must have been just over the horizon. If they'd sailed almost directly east, they would have passed within 20 miles of Nauru and as little as 15 from Ocean Island.

Taking account of prevailing winds and currents and the distance they'd traversed since sighting Nauru, Captain DaRosa calculated that they had traveled about 33 or 34 miles per day. After passing Nauru they'd continued into eastern Micronesia, where they must have sailed clear through the middle of the Kiribati islands. Although Kiribati spreads across an area that consists mainly of water, a deviation in their course of just five degrees left or right would have enabled them to make a landfall on one of the 14 islands—seven to the south and seven to the north of their route—that comprise the country. They must have passed between the islands of Aranuka and Nonouti, and were perhaps less than 10 miles from Nonouti at some point.

But if the *Evelina DaRosa* hadn't picked them up when it did, in a few more days they would have left the western fishing zone of the Pacific, where boats are relatively numerous, into the empty Central Pacific. They would not have entered the eastern fishing zone off the South American coast for at least another 100 days. In all likelihood they would have not survived for that long.

"So how was it that you found us in the middle of that emptiness?" Vince asked. "Why were you there in that place?"

"You ask why my ship was at that spot. Well, I will show you," DaRosa replied, walking toward a framed picture hanging on the rear wall of the pilot house.

"It was because of Him," he said, pointing to a person in the picture. "He led me to you; He guided me. That's how!"

The two men gazed at the picture, speechless. It depicted a sailor at his ship's helm, in the grip of a terrible storm. His eyes showed determination and courage. But he needed more to survive the storm. Right behind him stood another seaman; resting one hand upon the shoulder of the helmsman and with the other pointing the way, guiding the ship to shelter and safety. Below the picture was the caption: *Christ my Navigator*.

The men stood in silence a moment longer, eyes brimming, thinking about the miracle that this Navigator had performed in *their* lives.

～

Right then the five may have been safe, but they were still a long way from home. They needed a lot of care before they would be fit to make that journey. Although they were in good spirits, physically they were still in bad shape.

During the three days of the voyage to Kiribati the five enjoyed the hospitality of *Evelina*'s crew. They had a special room furnished with only a table, chair, and their mattresses. On the wall, written in English, were the words "God's Room." After being so near death, it surely was heaven. In fact it was the ship's prayer room—a place where the crew and officers could go for prayer or meditation. The men took the opportunity to make the most of it, continuing their morning and evening worships.

One night it came up in conversation as to just how

close the drifters in their boat had come to being ignored by the *Evelina*. Captain DaRosa told them of how they'd planned to turn away until Carlos the mastman saw someone waving to the *Evelina* from their dinghy.

"But no one waved to you from our boat," Vince responded, confused. "We did not see you until you were just a few yards away!"

"But someone waved," DaRosa said. "If he hadn't, we would have ignored you."

"Then the explanation is clear," Vince answered. "I say it was our guardian angel that you saw. We were all busy in the back of our boat with thoughts of Cleveland and completing our morning worship. We did not wave—it was another miracle."

The night before the *Evelina* docked in Kiribati the crew put on a party for the five survivors. They had cake and ice-cream—as much as they could eat—and gifts. The men received *Evelina DaRosa* T-shirts and then were "initiated" into the ranks of her crew. The former castaways celebrated with singing and laughter, and in turn toasted the good fortune of the men of the *Evelina*. But they also spent a minute in silence in honor of the memory of Cleveland and his grieving family.

Captain DaRosa felt that he needed to say something to the five men before he left them on Tarawa. But not sure what to tell them, he slipped into his cabin, and after a prayer for guidance, took his Bible from its place on the shelf. It fell open to the book of James and chapter 1. His eye was drawn to verse 12, and he wrote it down. Back in the mess he passed it to Joses who read it to the group: "Blessed is the man who endures temptation; for when he has been proved, he will receive the crown of life which the Lord promised to those who love Him."

It was the perfect message from a loving God for any who endure trial.

Captain DaRosa had the men tidied up for their arrival. They had haircuts and a shave, and put on clothing donated by the crew. Now, as a parting gift, as if rescuing them wasn't enough, he handed them US$300 for expenses plus a pair of sheets for each of them. The next morning they docked in Bairiki, on Tarawa. Awaiting them was an Australian naval officer, a shipping agent, an immigration officer, half a dozen government officials, a doctor, and ambulance attendants.

After greeting the castaways, the delegation then informed them that if they brought their boat ashore, it would be confiscated. The islanders talked about this together for a few moments, then turned to Captain DaRosa. He and his crew should keep it as a gift, they said.

DaRosa hesitated for a moment, then graciously accepted the battered, weather-beaten dinghy—but promised to return it if ever he visited Emirau.

The *Evelina* still had fish to catch, and the long detour had cost it a lot of time and money. So, reluctantly, just two hours later the crew made their farewells, and as the five men rode off in an ambulance, the *Evelina* vanished back into the haze of the blue Pacific.

The five were overjoyed to feel sand between their toes once again. But sadness tempered the happiness of their arrival when later that day they attended the funeral of their *wantok* and companion Cleveland. Although his body had been preserved in the cool-room of the *Evelina*, the morgue on Tarawa was having problems with its re-frigeration unit. In the heat of the tropics a body quickly decomposes, so once off-loaded from the ship, it was nec-essary to inter the body as soon as possible.

Cleveland was buried in a sandy grave in the town cemetery. After the brief service presented by Pastor Biribo Kabaneiti, the local Seventh-day Adventist minis-ter, the five survivors returned to the hospital. Later in the week they had a headstone placed on the grave. Many local well-wishers visited the grave and left flowers.

The strongest of the men were soon transferred to the Ocean Tide Hotel, where, after eating their fill, they slept in comfortable beds. Joses and Grosby stayed in the hospital until the end of the week, when their strength returned.

Surprises filled their stay in Kiribati. They received visits from local dignitaries, including the Minister for Foreign Affairs; gave interviews on local radio; and re-ceived a stream of invitations from homes, schools, and community and church groups to tell their story. The people treated them as visiting celebrities or officials.

They spent another week feted around the island while they waited for their travel arrangements to be made. It was to be a convoluted and time-consuming journey home, but that only served to raise the level of anticipation.

Finally they boarded an Air Nauru Boeing 737 bound for Fiji. The first leg took them due south, even further from home. In Suva they stayed in a comfortable hotel for the weekend awaiting their Sunday-morning connec-tion to Honiara, in the Solomon Islands, to their northwest. After a short transit at the Henderson Field, the international airport for Honiara, they boarded an Air Niugini F28 for an hour-long flight to Port Moresby. At around midday they touched down at Jacksons Airport.

In Port Moresby they spent an entire week celebrating with their Emirau *wantoks*, then, more than a month after rescue, they boarded another F28 for the final hop across the Owen Stanleys and Bismarck Sea to Kavieng, where four months before their ill-fated journey had begun.

At Kavieng Airport the excitement generated by all the anticipation reached a climax. Preparation for their arrival had begun almost the moment that Derrol Maisi heard the report of their rescue. As an Emirau administrator, it was Derrol's job to ensure that all parties were satisfied with the arrangements. Because Cleveland wasn't coming home, some didn't want a big public welcome. But others thought that it was a good opportunity to rekindle the spirit of unity, the absence of which they blamed for the troubles that had recently befallen Emirau.

But as it was going to be difficult to repress the joy and excitement—it was already bursting out—the community decided to make the arrival a festive event, but one that showed respect for Cleveland and his bereaved family. After what the five survivors had been through, the island reasoned that a public welcome would help their recovery and adjustment. Most of all, personal and political conflicts would be put aside as the whole community came together to welcome back those who once had been assumed dead but were now alive!

The little F28 taxied to the Kavieng Airport terminal, rocked to a halt, then the door opened. As the five former castaways stepped from the plane, they were overwhelmed by what they saw. Hundreds of people crowded the tiny terminal and lawns, and people lined the road into Kavieng. A line of dignitaries and officials wending from the steps of the plane to the door of the terminal waited to formally greet them. Among them were the province's chief administrator, Lima Dotocona; national government MP, Paul Tohian; the provincial police commander, Philip Solala; the director of Emergency Services for the province; the Harbors Board manager; the chairman of the Murat local government; and a host of Seventh-day Adventist Church ministers, leaders, and members.

But most important among those forming the reception party were the families of the men. They included Vince's sister, Lynnete Kavale; Joses's sister, Lydia Phinias; Donald's sister, Warina Reinard; Grosby's brother, Seth Ume; Titus's grandfather, Pastor Lauvos; and Cleveland's sister, Wenny Glan.

After tears, hugs, and a few short speeches, they drove in convoy the mile into Kavieng town. Up until then everyone had been fairly quiet. The thought of the one who had not made it had a sobering effect on everyone. But the conflicting emotions of grief and happiness inside them begged for release. The quiet lasted while the men walked from the cars to the front of the large tent set up for the meeting. Then, as children presented them with flowers, the audience erupted, clapping and singing but also into tears!

All afternoon speeches followed more speeches. Finally the honored guests and well-wishers moved to tables piled high with food and the real celebration began. The men gave their account of the journey, which the people greeted with cheers and clapping. People congratulated the men for keeping their faith and for never giving up hope. Eventually, as the sun began to set and when everyone had eaten their fill, they began to drift home, leaving the men to spend time alone with their *wantoks*.

"It was a remarkable event," Derrol Maisi said later. "I just cannot forget it. And peace and cooperation has pervaded our island since then. We learned the hard way that you can fail together, but you also can win together.

"Even though we have many trials in life, we must encourage each other. We must always stand together."

CHAPTER
13

BREAD CAST ON DEEP WATERS

The celebration for the return of the five drifters might have been over, but the saga was not yet complete.

On Wednesday, April 5, 1998, just a few months after he'd organized the homecoming in Kavieng, Derrol Maisi, received another radio message from Kavieng Emergency Services.

"You need to come over here," it said. "We have a drifter! He's in a bad way, and we're bringing him to Kavieng Hospital from New Hanover. We do not know who he is, and we're not sure of where he's come from, but we think it might be Kiribati!"

Derrol left his work on Emirau and caught a boat to Kavieng, where he went directly to the Emergency Services office to get a more complete story.

A few days earlier, the duty officer explained, a small aluminum dingy with a 25-horsepower motor had washed onto a beach on Mansava, a tiny island off the northern coast of New Hanover. The boat contained two people. They had obviously been at sea for a long time, as thirst and exposure had killed one and the other, although alive, was close to death. A local islander, one William Freeman, had discovered the boat.

He'd initially cared for the survivor, then when the man had somewhat recovered, had taken him and the body to Taskul, a small town on the island of New Hanover where there was a government aid post. Its nursing staff had placed the castaway on an IV drip until he had recovered sufficiently for transfer to the better equipped Kavieng Hospital. No one had been able to talk with him, because of his poor physical state and an obvious language difficulty.

Would Derrol try to communicate with him and discover his origins? Emergency Services asked.

"Of course," Derrol agreed, and left immediately for the hospital to meet his new responsibility.

As Derrol looked at the emaciated skeleton that lay in the bed, thoughts of recent events flooded back. Despite the ravages of deprivation and exposure that had so grotesquely altered the man's appearance, his hair and facial features strongly suggested that he was from Kiribati. As a first step toward establishing his origin, Derrol drew a series of pictures of objects from various parts of the Pacific, indicating that he should confirm if he was familiar with each of them. The man shook his head or nodded as Derrol drew fruit, vegetables, and fish of various species, and a host of other objects. Eventually Derrol was able to deduce that the man was, in fact, from Kiribati.

Once it became generally known that the man was from Kiribati, people began to say that as a reciprocal token of their appreciation for what his island had done for the Emirau castaways, the people of Emirau, and Kavieng's Seventh-day Adventist community in particular, should take responsibility for the drifter and the funeral of his dead *wantok*.

Derrol left the hospital and went back to the Emergency Services office where he radioed the situation to his Emirau *wantoks*. He asked them if they would take care of the funeral. Could they weave funeral mats and send them to Kavieng?

Someone told him about a Kiribati islander who was a student at Pacific Adventist University (PAU), the Seventh-day Adventist university in Port Moresby. An officer of the provincial administration contacted the man, Danny Langley, and asked him to fly to Kavieng immediately.

Danny arrived the following Saturday morning. He went directly to the hospital where he spoke with the man, who was now almost recovered, and confirmed Derrol's conclusion. Speaking through Danny, the man told Derrol of his terrible ordeal.

Originally there'd been three of them in the boat—the owner and his son, and himself. They'd come all the way from Kiribati. The owner had only just purchased the boat, so decided to try it on the open sea. They were fishing when a rainstorm blew in and obscured the land. The islands of Kiribati are all extremely low-lying and virtually invisible at even a short distance from low down. They'd motored this way and that, searching, until their fuel ran out, then drifted at the mercy of the west-flowing current, with virtually no food or fresh water, to

PNG. They'd been at sea for about three months.

It all sounded familiar to Derrol. Like the six men from Emirau, this trio had experienced dreadful privation, mental and physical torture, and unending thirst.

Eventually, physically and mentally weakened, they'd yielded to the temptation to drink seawater. The son became sick and died, and the bereaved father began to lose hope. Eventually he lost his reason. They were so weak, that even together, they couldn't lift the decomposing body of the dead boy over the dinghy side for burial. Discouragement so overcame the father that he decided to end it all. He crawled over the gunwales, and despite the pleading of the other survivor, dropped into the water, hoping to drown.

Tears welled in the eyes of the Kiribati man as he recounted how, once in the water, his friend realized his peril and the finality of what he was doing. He called for help and struggled to climb back into the boat. But so weakened were they, that between them they hadn't sufficient strength to get him back in. The man lost his grip on the dinghy and, as it continued to drift along on the light breeze, the other drifter watched his friend fall further astern of the boat, futilely struggling to stay afloat. That was the last time he saw him, for moments later he disappeared below a wave and didn't resurface. The body in the boat was the man's son.

What made the tragedy more poignant was that it had occurred just a day or so before the boat washed onto Mansava Island. The man could have made it, if only he hadn't given up.

On, Sunday, April 19, 1998, Joses and Titus were

among those who carried the casket of the dead Kiribati boy from the ambulance to its resting place in Kavieng's cemetery. The funeral, paradoxically, was really something of a high day in Kavieng. Although everyone was respectful of the dead boy and the survivor, here was an opportunity to repay their debt to the people of Kiribati.

The police had escorted the procession as it had wended its way from the hospital to the cemetery. The ambulance had carried the casket, then came Danny Langley representing Kiribati, and behind him followed officers of the provincial government, Derrol Maisi, and a crowd of onlookers, including many from Emirau.

People placed specially woven mats on the grave and the casket, in the tradition of their culture. Some of the mats they buried with the Kiribati lad, but others they retrieved and presented to Danny with instructions to leave them on Cleveland's grave in Kiribati when he returned home. This he promised to do.

Despite the fact that no one who attended the funeral knew the deceased, it was still charged with emotion. In everyone's mind was the thought of young Cleveland, buried so far from his home, on remote Kiribati. "We felt that as we had one of our *wantoks* buried in this man's homeland of Kiribati, now this man from Kiribati was buried in ours," Derrol Maisi explained. "Sadly, we repaid our debt to the people of Kiribati in kind."

But the circle was complete.

∼

From the time of their return to Kavieng, and especially on Emirau, people viewed the drifters as celebrities and heroes. Two months is usually about the limit for survival adrift, and they'd lasted three. Despite their indifference toward religion during their earlier lives, they'd learned the value of a faith and now lived it. They'd experienced supernatural intervention in their lives. It's not surprising that today the five are more closely bonded than any *wantok* relationship.

The men endured great hardship together, yet through their determination to never give up they survived.

CHAPTER
14

POSTSCRIPT

On Tarawa Captain DaRosa had reluctantly accepted the gift of the drifters' boat. And before he departed the dock on Tarawa he had said he would return it if he could. In fact, from the time he left Kiribati for the fishing fleet, the thought became an obsession.

Some six months later DaRosa kept his word. He pointed the 1,600-ton *Evelina DaRosa* westward and headed for Papua New Guinea, specifically Emirau Island. During the interim the crew of the *Evelina* had completely refurbished the little boat, scraping and painting the hull while the ship's carpenter added some comfortable varnished wooden seats and trim.

The *Evelina* arrived off Emirau at daybreak, after the longest voyage she'd ever undertaken. They couldn't see a jetty, dock, or harbor, so they dropped anchor well offshore. DaRosa stepped into his onboard Hughes 5000 helicopter normally used for fish spotting and flew to a village a few hundred yards inland where he hovered overhead as people came running to greet him.

"We landed on a makeshift landing strip and asked a child where we could get our skiff ashore. A girl pointed toward a sheltered cove. I went back to the ship, and we launched the skiff and the drifter's boat and went in.

"Now the whole village came out to meet us, everyone cheering and crying at once. Unfortunately we only got to see Titus, as the other drifters were off the island. I hardly recognized him. He'd put on about 50 pounds— in fact, he was quite chubby!

"The villagers were very gracious and gave us presents of squash, melons, coconuts, and pumpkins. They wanted us to stay longer, but we could afford only three or four hours, then had to leave."

So the 12-week saga of six young men adrift in an open boat ended.

Captain DaRosa did ask Joe his navigator why he'd altered the *Evelina*'s course. Joe said that he set the course at 225° (not 205°) because that was the course Captain DaRosa had given him. Captain DaRosa still cannot recall issuing such an order.